Gova

Ike Mboneni Muila

First published in 2004 by Botsotso Publishing
Box 23910 Joubert Park 2044
botsotso@artslink.co.za

Acknowledgements

On that fly page wangu for the so-called poetry book Gova: Muvenda Journal, Bliksem, donga, New Coin, Poetry of the 90s, Something Quarterly, Triple C Poetry, Tripwire, Gekko Poetry, Staffrider, Imprint, Botsotso Publishing, and others...

Second Imprint: 2009

ISBN: 978-0-6398785-1-5

The publisher would like to thank the Roy Joseph Cotton Poetry Trust for its support.

Layout and design by Nadine Botha

contents

Other titles by Botsotso Publishing

Botsotso, an annual literary magazine

Poetry

We Jive Like This
Botsotso Jesters
(Siphiwe ka Ngwenya, Isabella Motadinyane, Allan Kolski Horwitz, Ike Mboneni Muila, Anna Varney)

No Free Sleeping
Donald Parenzee, Vonani Bila, Alan Finlay

Dirty Washing
Botsotso Jesters

5
Clinton Du Plessis, Kobus Moolman, Gillian Schutte, Bofelo wa Mphutlane, Lionel Murcott

Purple Light Mirror in the Mud (compact disc)
Botsotso Jesters and Lionel Murcott
(a joint production with 111)

Short fiction

Unity in Flight
Maropodi Mapalakanye, Peter Rule, Zachariah Rapola, Michael Vines, Phaswane Mpe, Allan Kolski Horwitz

Un/common Ground
Allan Kolski Horwitz

Post-Traumatic: New South African Short Stories
Edited by Chris van Wyk

Art

Manuscript Exhibition 2000

Manuscript Exhibition 002

Gova

Ike Mboneni Muila's Mix Masala that says, Jump On, Welcome Aboard!

The word-wand weaves images that translate from our Experience. Conducted by Imagination, they become part of the sensual world – the world of hard and soft knocks, perfumes and stenches. In the 1950's, the so-called "tsotsi taal" of the townships, the slang used by the most marginalised - the criminals and the artists - developed in response to the innate hunger that all people have to express themselves, and to do so in the language that most reflects themselves and their world. So it was, in a spirit of defiance and verve that all the languages spoken in the polyglot Black ghettoes were incorporated into an urban argot that became known as Isicamtho. Out of the 'mix and marry' of new expressions a vibrant bridge crossed chasms in all directions. A language that embraces all the diverse heritages of our fractured society – that is surely a creation to treasure!

Such is the word-wand that Ike Mboneni Muila plays with – and play is the word, for isicamtho is above all a joyous and tongue-in-cheek 'grootbek' of a lingo. With respect to its inimitable juiciness, it often strikes me as being a relative of Yiddish, that other extraordinary hybrid of languages. And Ike as a master practitioner conjures the craziness into subconscious order. The train of his associations screaming across our minds, awakening in turn our own further associations – transformed and transforming. So for those who are not intimately acquainted with Isicamtho one can only advise – dive in! Do not get stuck on individual words/expressions – plunge head first into the maelstrom. Only then will you break the language barrier! Of course, those who are long time wasekaya or bandiete, will appreciate the subtleties, the finer points, and savour. But first-timers too will taste the fruits with great delight

jump on

as I and many others have over the years till we became more and more attuned - not just to the words themselves but to the rhythms and the intonations.

Given the South African tendency to be dominated by other imperial cultures (once European, now North American) Ike Mboneni Muila stands out as a South African original – not that he is the first to write in Isicamtho (many others have done so), but that he is the first to build a developed body of work that is entirely in Isicamtho and makes no apology for that. How refreshing to hear his work in the middle of the hip-hop/rap bombardment or the pseudo-Rasta talk and spelling affected by so many young and not-so young poets! Yes, Isicamtho is best experienced live, in performance. The words flow like a tide, musical to their core. In this regard, the compact disk accompanying this book captures the irrepressible energy of the poems that a quiet reading on the page cannot do. Indeed, a very considerable attraction of the book is the CD – especially in its capturing of Ike's unique voice.

And so it is. The situations and emotions on which his poems are based remain individual, yet carry the imprint of wider social influences. And both the style and content challenge orthodoxy and comfort. Small wonder that the esteemed but out-of-touch anthologists of South African poetry do not take the trouble to properly engage with Ike's work. And when they do so, they show their condescension, and fail to identify the most powerful, the most vital. As such a definitive anthology of contemporary South African poetry is still very much lacking. Indeed, witness the ongoing inability to appreciate Wopko Jensma, one of our most innovative and profound poets.

Ike's early work published in the 1990's in the Botsotso Jester poetry books, WE JIVE LIKE THIS and DIRTY WASHING, established his presence. This collection takes that work several steps further. May you enjoy the ride!

Allan Kolski Horwitz

Johannesburg/Jozi

greetings emsawawa

we molo
abusheni hola
mangwanani
sanibonani thovhela
ri - ya - losha
welele ebukhosini bakhiwa hola
sharp hoezit moja
to my dear friend
brothers en sisters
at heart
hasalaam alaikum
malaikum salaam ..,
goodlord gordsave the queen
the one en only queen like candle in the wind
for insinuating a war monger beast
in that bush of united states of america
both americans juju monkey do monkey see
now lord a poem
after the myth
inside of me

stomach ulcer complications 1 side a (i)

stomach ulcer complications 27/01/03

on the day i received sad news of her sudden death in a clinic hospital orange farm. i was shuttered i felt stomach butterflies running all over the show then i felt something rising towards my throat and there i was speechless and howling like a dog without it's bone. isabella motadinyane was born on the 17th feb 1963 mofolo central and passed away suffering from a death of speech in a hospital clinic orange farm on the 19th jan 2003. she wrote a poem that gave birth to botsotso publishers and botsotso poetry performers as botsotso jesters i met isabella while a stage manager in their workshop play about life in theatre pimville of the early sixties of gangsterims, music and social politics of that time even the tsotsitaal lingo used at that particular times under the title skom short for skomplaas that is emzini.., at home .., during tea time and lunch time we would be discussing creative writing that is poetry and state drama performance complementing each other she became my soul mate and she told me to throw away my walking stick which i used to keep my body up..,

right while struggling with the force of gravity since my permanent brain fracture blow i suffered in 91 jeppe street jozi, i wrote her a poem my better half..,

she also told me of her sad story that she believed in she told me that she wont live longer because of her stomach ulcer complication she told me her mother took her to a family planning clinic for sterile and birth control while she was a young school kid for fear of unwanted pregnancy she told me her tubes got blocked and that led to her life threatening..,

stomach

1 b side (ii)

ulcer complications

stomach sore pains which would finally take her life, to me she was such a strong sister soldier and a fighter who does not easily bow down to minor pains then she would curl up in bed next to me giving me squeaky sound of ehchu.., ehchu farting and laughing hysterical when i ask her why was that she would tell me the pain is gone out with the fart we would both laugh hysterical while she.., continues to fart i would hold her kiss her and then ask her what she would love to drink before and after meal as a wash down she would tell me she is tired of drinking white waters that is milk sugar and hot water as her one and only tea she would love to drink beer and be merry waya waya to entertain the mass of poetry lovers with a beer in a hand drinking like nobody's business and with our own creative writing coming home with raving reviews i could now remember vividly she creatively wrote sink a shaft.., before a beer bottle while we were rehearsing poetry and spontaneously collectively creating and recreating folk songs that would go along with the poetry in grahamstown poetry festival perfomance - since 1993 to 98 after an evening performance we would go to the nearest wimpy bar or favourite pub to rewind chanting poetry brains storming and discussing possible channels for our creative effort and going to sleep after hours making sure no matter how much drunk we could be that we wake up on time to take a shower or a warm bath during our collective effort she would come up with melody and then –

stomach ulcer complication

c side 1 (iii)

we would sit down jointly work on the lyrics and finally write down the folk songs for example vulani song bonang wee bantwana song written and recorded in the 1995 performance poetry festival video grahamstown with isabella in rhodes university video title 'jikeleza train.., which gave birth to wordfest.., isabella motadinyane was a born genius she went as far as grade five at school a highly spiritual person chosen by her ancestrors to serve them as a songoma to be.., if you argue or disagree without any valid reasonable point.., uya doya you fail dismal she would put you to shame and prove you wrong on the spot and make you feel stupid she does not care whether you are white or black makhulu baas or top shaela.., academic bra.., at school she memorised a narrative from the unknown author "the extract from the dangerous ground" which she could beautifully chant word for word with such a marvellous understanding to me she was an extra ordinary singer, dancer, poet, actress, performer, a unique soul mate and we use to influence each other in one way or the other at times we could stay away from drinking for six to seven weeks period during that time facing the harshness of life reality.., sober minded in pains she would come to me and say that there is.., some thing which is running from her stomach to her throat and choking her making it difficult for her to breath.., and you could see her hopeless pale face and that she is in a pensive mood and loosing weight and then she would go on for weeks praying and taking instructions from her ancestors consulting with christian prophets sangomas friends for

stomach ulcer complications

d side 1 (iv)

advice then slowly she would regain her weight and her face looking brighter she would come up with those ehchu.., ehchu sound farting and we would both laugh hysterical that the pain is gone out with the fart then we will resume our normal eat and drinking spree when she is good and ready in her pretty mood with her strong spiritual belief she would say to me amongst her ancestors she is guided by three outstanding characters a christian prophet a sangoma and an aggressive dumb founded instructor who facilitate messages amongst chrisian prophet and sangomas a dumbfounded.., character usually visit her when she is on a beer drinking spree and also come in on a special visit or a call to deliver and facilitate an assignment amongst people she use to work with practice or help or assist she could not charge on her own accord her patients she could only go along with what they give her as long as at the end of the day she could afford a beer to console her self and rejoice and that use to make me feel sad and disoriented because even people in the arts in the creative writing and poetry performances people just want to be entertained mahala free bees they just don't feel like to pay or buy products of the arts they don't care what you eat at the end of the day or.., how you make a living - they just don't have respect for our creative efforts as artist and that is why we perish invain and so poor without anyone who cares a damn at the end of the day jikelele..

wangu dear ike

wangu dear ike
waaren hoe is jy nou die tyd
jump tyd humours dorp
geen moratowa naby die kant for dice
ou matwetwe ngulevhe spy
haba haba njalaza humours dorp
or kanjani tsa ..,
where are my love letters ?
i keep on sending you to no avail
shiyabuya ike ..,
i believe you believe

that we all believe you are
what you write about
baby you are a tsotsi
in a tsotsitaal skin mjucate
where did we go wrong
in those sweet moments of love
skuwet under corset
humoursdorp hanging on the edge of eternity
bambezela tsotsi siya jika
corner crash travelling rugs veranda stoep no dice
hoor net daar mjucate

my man is madly in love ringas wise
i mean in love with the so called tsotsitaal
isicamtho wasekhaya
kindly do return my love regards
in a witty lingo half moja ek se..,
of hoese ek nou die laste madala site caution
welele wele wele wela wela
yours sincere ncasment
umaqumbane
x love in disarray

buddy scamtho

buddy scamtho

buddy scamtho
first and fore most i accept and thank you
for your invitation
with my most humble beginnings
buddy scamtho jam
nwana mme smoko
kasie prent shosholoza style
khoma switiya nwana mmani
spyker hammer chisel foloza mkokoteli
dish dash pozi jinda warm ginsa lapha site
skokkend werk liya shisa emsawawa cowsin
i am into creative writing as a poet artist performer
my narrative oral mix is in eleven
languages spoken in south africa
by and bye trapped in one poem
the so called tsotsitaal isicamtho lingo alive
and kicking sense of humour in you and me
mixing of languages into a witty lingo
a language of identity
a language of an ordinary person in the street
a language of unity in diversity

matakadza mbilu ! ndi nwana
chu chu baby ! ndi nwana
talk talk baby ! ndi nwana
cry cry baby ! ndi nwana
ah, ah baby ! ndi nwana
oh, oh, baby ! ndi nwana

a song matakadza mbilu is a folk song by
the malende dance culture which says what brings
happiness to the heart is a child
in this instance
the ultimate child
in my case
is isicamtho

bottle kop shova

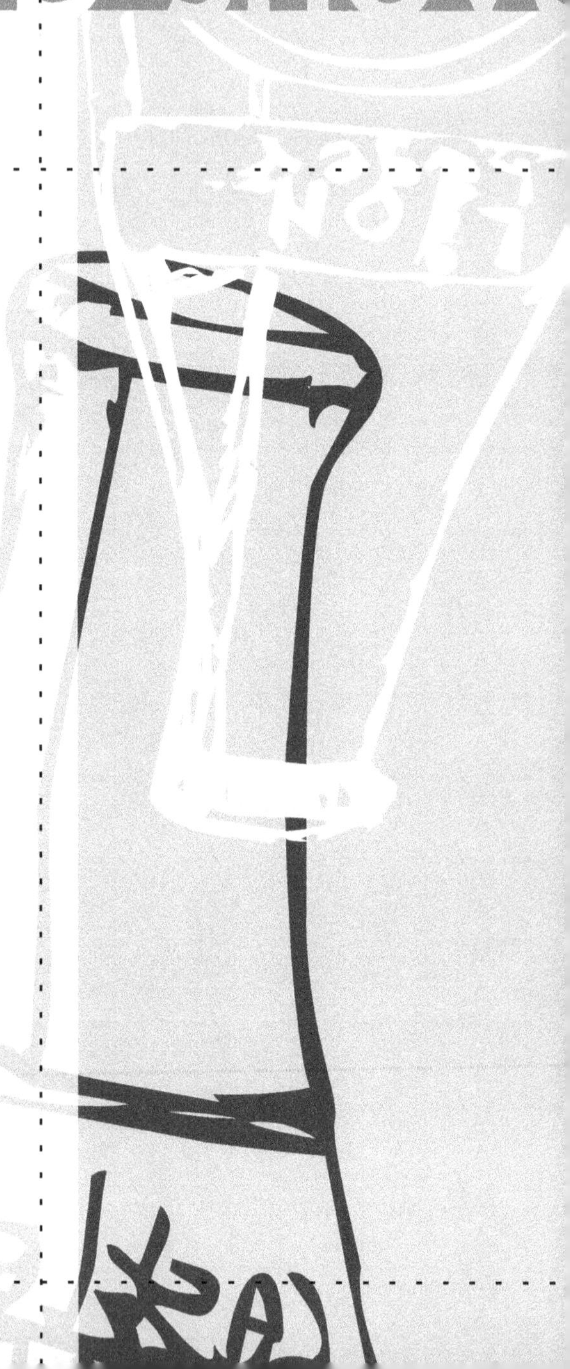

bottle kop shova
sprinkane outfit bars
disturbance – woza – woza meet the eye
wholesaler rap strictly casual dakota fluit
snuff box phashane tennis shoe shine khaki
muddy plastic hot hit mateki smelling socks
harrow ruik for bidden fox thoasa pepe
thiza ntanjane file reading goggle sgele
kopa dungarees goal keeper fence
ziya mporoma kabo maseven for life
toetsa spy kos gimba captain
die ander kant baya chuchurumbisa
bottle kopshova
boere wors en tea bone steak braai
kom kry toast gimba so maar gooi
en swallow chisa nyama
madala site javas get real
umdubulo we fong kong wat gat aan
party line plastic figure penny penny guy foxy
bambino case open en close chapter verse van
gooi om en gooi weg mindless taste
gova burst.., morning after mbizo bells
bottle kop shova
three artificial body parts
false tande couple gimmicks binne bathroom toilet
digging an anglo sex language poem
back round bottle kop shova camera rol
action…

jack in a bootleg

jack in a bootleg

durban line
telephone director tf
rook hulle mboza zol
half a jack nip
halakasha sweet brown sugar
so maar gooi dry yeast daar omtrent
spoon down test pass over patshutshu
hold me tight en let me move skhambathiwise
sandy hatch vuilskoene corner jive
ntonto dzingi dzingi mafula song
spinza nine la seven
hola mothers near the munombelo tree
fountain square
polipoli time keeper goalie off the wall
coolmate chomi thoasa
s.abrew
drievoet face quarter share
clean en green like
african dustbin caring a tree of liberty
that waters blood
of the martyr

side a (i)

autobiograph

to nazim hikmet

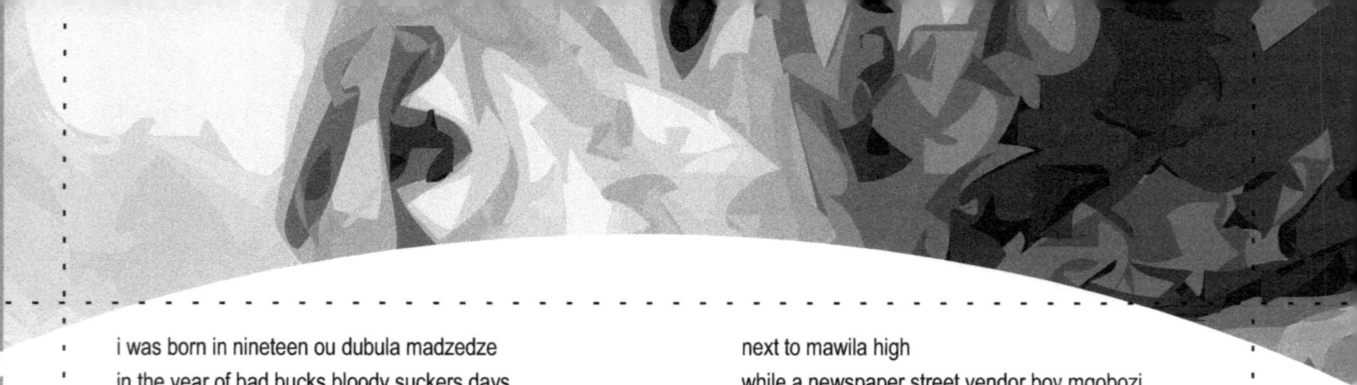

i was born in nineteen ou dubula madzedze
in the year of bad bucks bloody suckers days
at a mofolo village house in soweto
out of embaressment for others i lied too
I lied also so as not to hurt someone else
but i also lied for no apparent reason at all
i never really left my place of birth
i grew up wearing iwisa maize
mealie meal bag tshirt
green line shorts no dirty dozen under my feet
my feet never knew
or wore shoes at a tender age of eleven
until i was fifteen years old
still no dirty dozen under my feet
in fact you could hide a half-crown or fifty cent
under my rough cast concrete feet
called mukenke crocodile skin craks
no shoes no school nearby where i could learn my home language
emisebeni primary is where my intuition started to function in grade a
for my high school i went to meadowlands community school
next to mawila high
while a newspaper street vendor boy mgobozi
my neighbourly brother went to mawila high
school for xitsonga
for my senior secondary grade twelve sigele
i went to the northern province of limpopo venda
where my roots came from via the zambezi river
from the forceful removal of sophiatown
in 1955 my parents settled at a mofolo village house
in soweto where i was born
ike is my venda name colonized and sodomized
by the anglo-sex language
with empty promises
of heaven on earth
i believe you believe
that we all believe that ...,
mina nawe
nne na inwi
ri do ri ndi mbidi
nga u vhona mavhala

side b (ii)

autobiography
to nazim hikmet

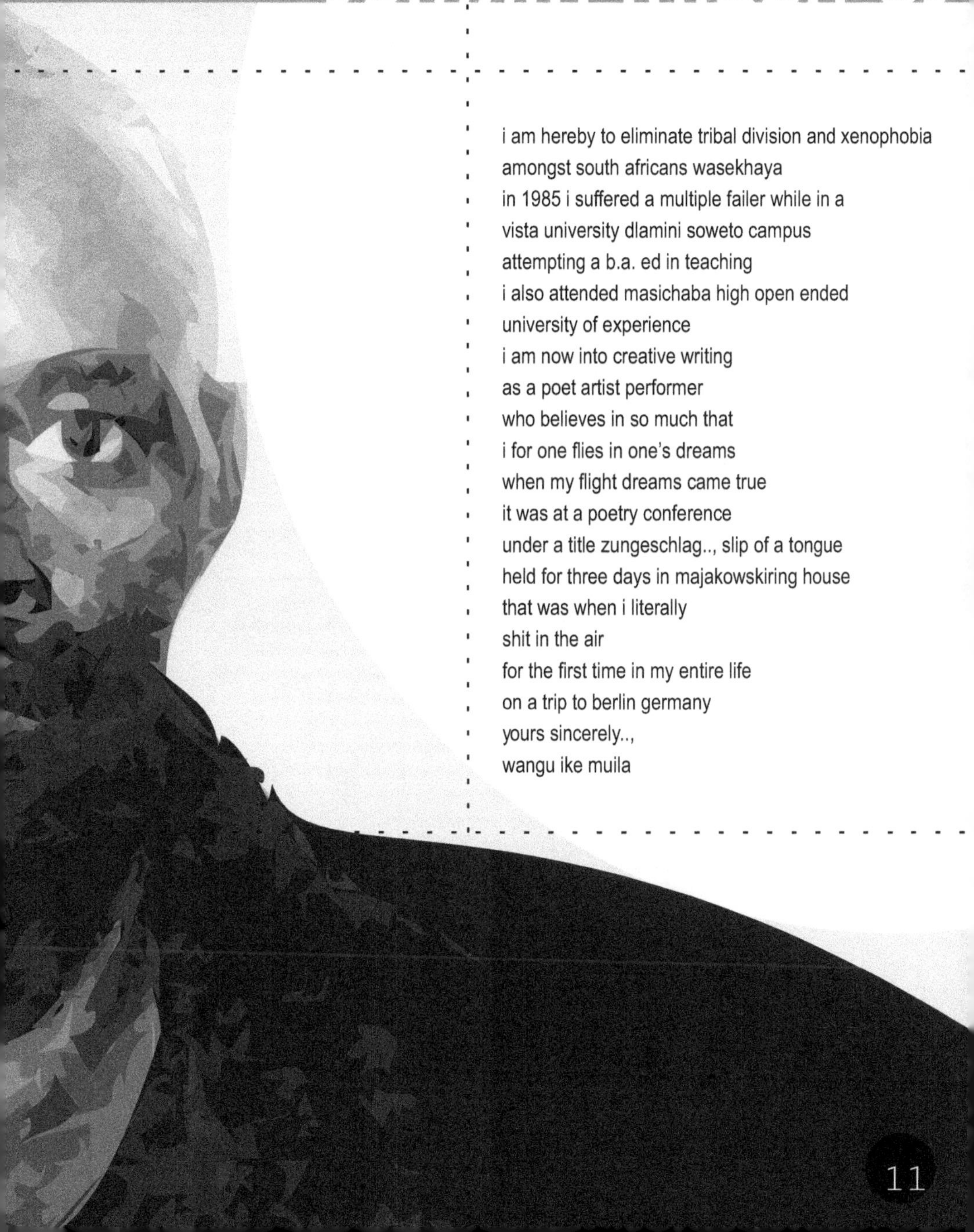

i am hereby to eliminate tribal division and xenophobia
amongst south africans wasekhaya
in 1985 i suffered a multiple failer while in a
vista university dlamini soweto campus
attempting a b.a. ed in teaching
i also attended masichaba high open ended
university of experience
i am now into creative writing
as a poet artist performer
who believes in so much that
i for one flies in one's dreams
when my flight dreams came true
it was at a poetry conference
under a title zungeschlag.., slip of a tongue
held for three days in majakowskiring house
that was when i literally
shit in the air
for the first time in my entire life
on a trip to berlin germany
yours sincerely..,
wangu ike muila

hide and seek

hide and seek gam

hide en seek game
black mapatile
no, no..,
banyana ba ipatile
no, no..,
amazambane.., awakavuthwa
amazambane.., awakavuthwa
mukuku.., mayi
mukuku.., mayi
how many.., ten
one two three four five
six seven eight nine ten
ngize.., no, no.., can i come
no, no.., ngize.., no, no..,
one two three block
                                one two three block
one two three block
                                out you go zwithi
kaufela on the spot
                                one two three block

saratoga
expres 06/06/y2k00...

aratoga express

06/06/y2koo..,

green caution
yellow red read
zaya saratoga express
divers no victory delivery
without casualty

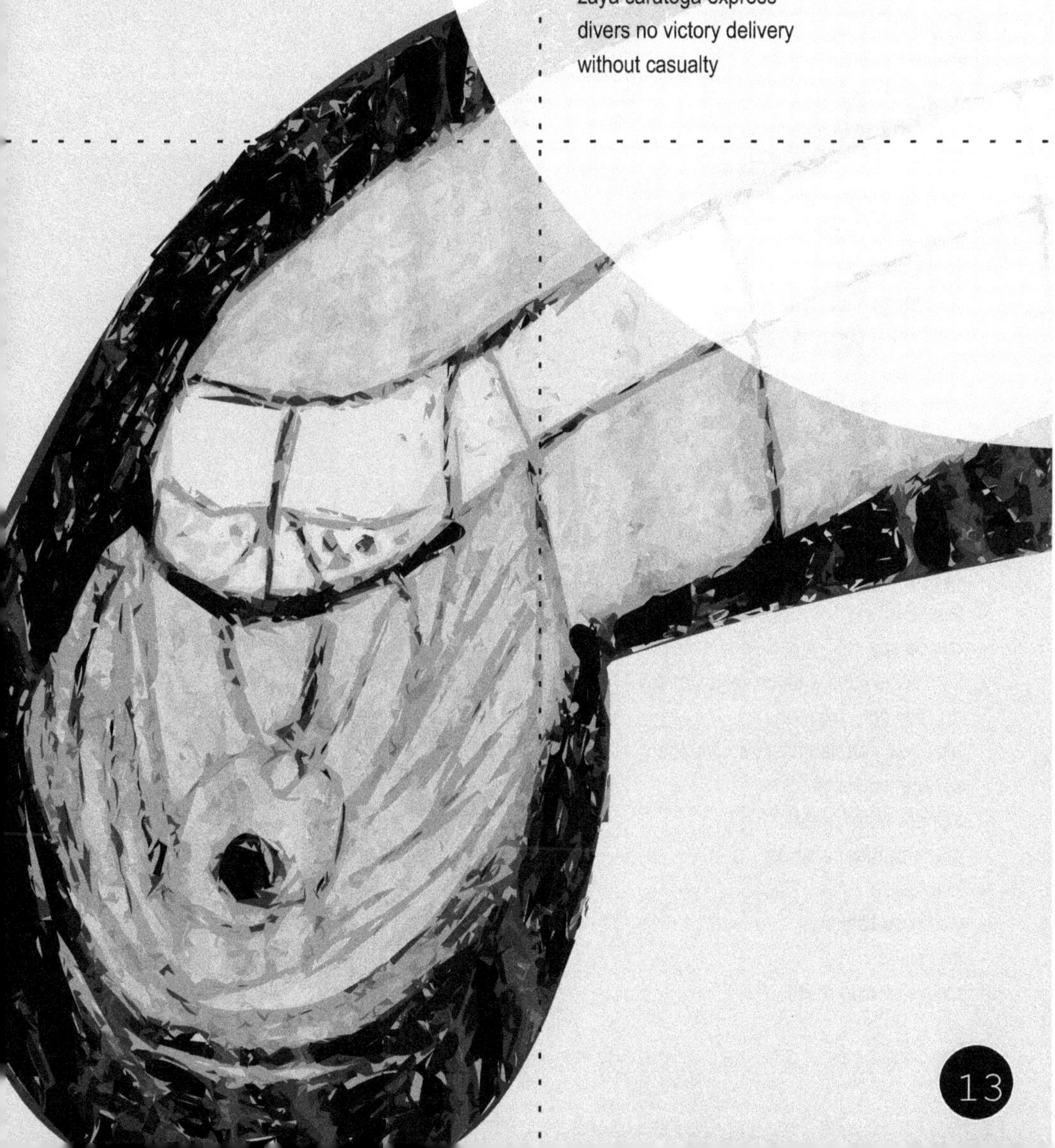

this poem

this poem ...,'

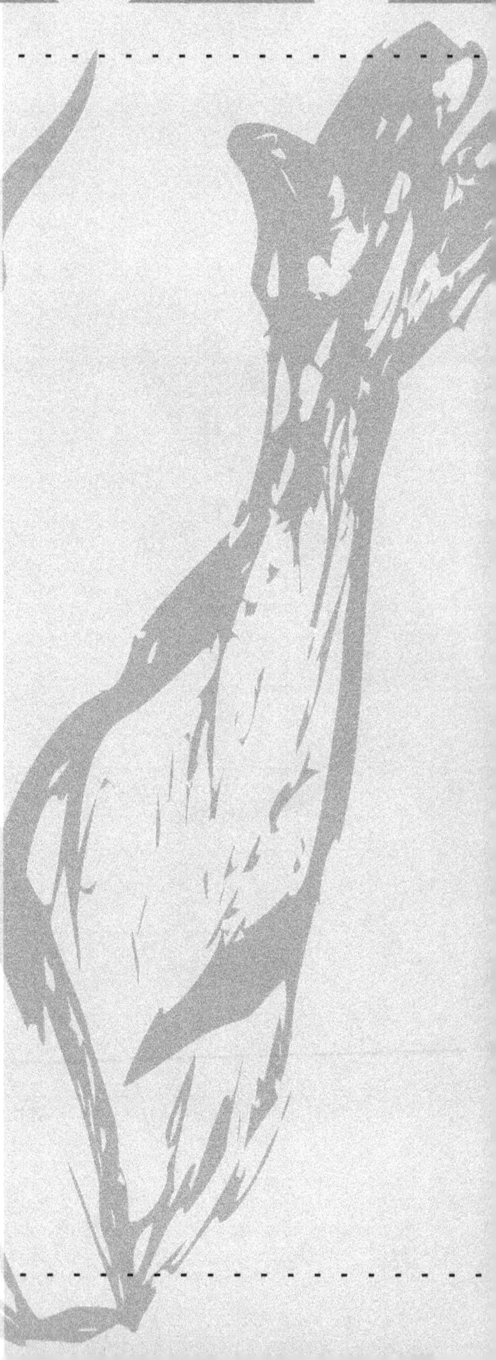

this poem ...,
is an extension of love index
blue mars trap
logger dancer
in between

- venus and mars
- umkhambathi archer stalk me
- inside out of an imaginary planet
- calabash logger dancer
- inkatha pot scraper spinach fence
- junior buck short
- love index of discomfort
- eloff street candy collar
- maravela
- corner market and nugget
- cake ndaba story pitika bova site
- washing brake coffee bar
- gauteng maboneng
- commissioner benrose
- ellispark calibres
- tapela
- tapepe spy
- kom kry skhumba touch salvation spy
- dry skin grace vaseline
- blue seal petroleum jelly stop station
- service touch line
- slander water proof
- dramatic order disorder
- in disguise
- wardrobe blinkers
- munching
- exclusive blue mass

1 side a (i)

i stare in wonder

i stare in wonder
stockings kilo meter bum jive grand
party house management pulling out
stinking boots en knicker bondage of the country
socks enticed by naked future feminique
sinking no strings attached
to love fencing spear head tumbler
within a bottomless maxosha shacks
unknown rough and ugly
ginger four manyawo pause a threat
to innocent heart broken container
i stare in wonder
jack roller without a heart driven gwavhavha
bo dae dairy fortress children of asazi kopa
i stare in wonder
kom kry huks vry staat get mchovana
spoon down test
the silver cup is broken
if you see a stop sign lapha site
shova take no u turn
qalaza syndicate then
short left or short right
waya waya niks mabuya joe
my brakate verstaan jy mnca
van die one one
jy slaat my dizzy wrong site
moen skokkend werk mabone jive
deedum dum dum
dummy table
i stare in wonder
them sluggish fat cow smoking a zol
bo dae joint outside the backyard wood
resembling them earring bulls without horns
sharing a blade in the ghetto jol

1 b side (ii)

stare in wonder

a drievoet face dose of marijuana
monkey do smoking a home made pipe
like a bottle kop shova
i stare in wonder
looking at mutavha-tsindi camp
nearby makonde mountain range
when it dawned in my mind
that a mother insectivorous plant does exist
which preys on anything alive even human beings
who dare go near by the tree
no wonder it is believed
you could only escape mutavhatsindi catch
if and only if you go nearby naked to the tree
i stare in wonder
failing to escape the loudness in my mind
my in law mulamu and i turned to listen
with all that funny feelings jogging in my mind
to bob marley's reggae music in a car
music with the philosophy of generations yet
to come by and ponder about war in the middle
east of nation war against nation
i stare in wonder still
cruising all over the mutale region
surrounded by the makonde mountain range
malondi and takalani in the back seat of a car
singing a venda version
of one of bob marley's songs
indeed..,
vha na gonova vha tshikhalani

side a (i)

pretty woman man ..,

side a (i)
pretty woman man ..

pretty woman man or man woman
either way kasie is die selde ding
dis mos nie bad om te guarantee chesterfield
delela samson strip strong rider overall vest
leather jacket jones en mafia shoes
kid sibali makoti pretty well
what a gay guy lesbian stem tide
to the powers that be
on a syndicate foxy line
of animal offal ngadealers coast
dish take eyeballs animal brains testicle
tongue livers hand to the traditional healers
pretty well thokoza makhosi
pretending a dynamics ngoma for life

private human body part mystery chemistry wise
in the traditional healers pretty get well industry
the marriage initiation failer to man woman
from macheke street eye witnesses
mathenga thenga buyisela o jile bhasela
a gay guy lesbian parade mahala bioscope
white wedding ululation from street corner to corner
a sudden door way steps fortune favour fools
tv scoop journalist gunning for the news break
at a mofolo village backyard house in soweto
a law suit pull triggers tamati sauce ellisa gegege
pretty oil defrauding sabc tv people for deformation of character
ubani mina ..,
wa mmbona wa nndivha

15 lines public poem

gone are the days
where i could be discovered
sitting like an artifact
in the middle of no where
as a centre of tourist attraction
under an all shame pity you
noise roofing container
behind a heavy notice board
written .., no jobs
azikho lomsebenzi
ku haba ntiro
famba kaya
mushumo au ho
people socialize creditable
gone are the days of wandering aimlessly

5 lines private poem

i better change my mind
i better change my mind
for good because mbilu ndi mbili
inwe ndi dala inwe ndi tsuku
the red heart reads run for dear life
do you see what gives and what takes pipeline
a green heart reads
to stay reap what you saw for life
relax calm down
a cry foul you pressed a wrong button
ask what wrong button have i pressed
is there anything missing dear jaws
what are you waiting for
still dreaming of the ojs coming
i better change my mind
i better change my mind for good

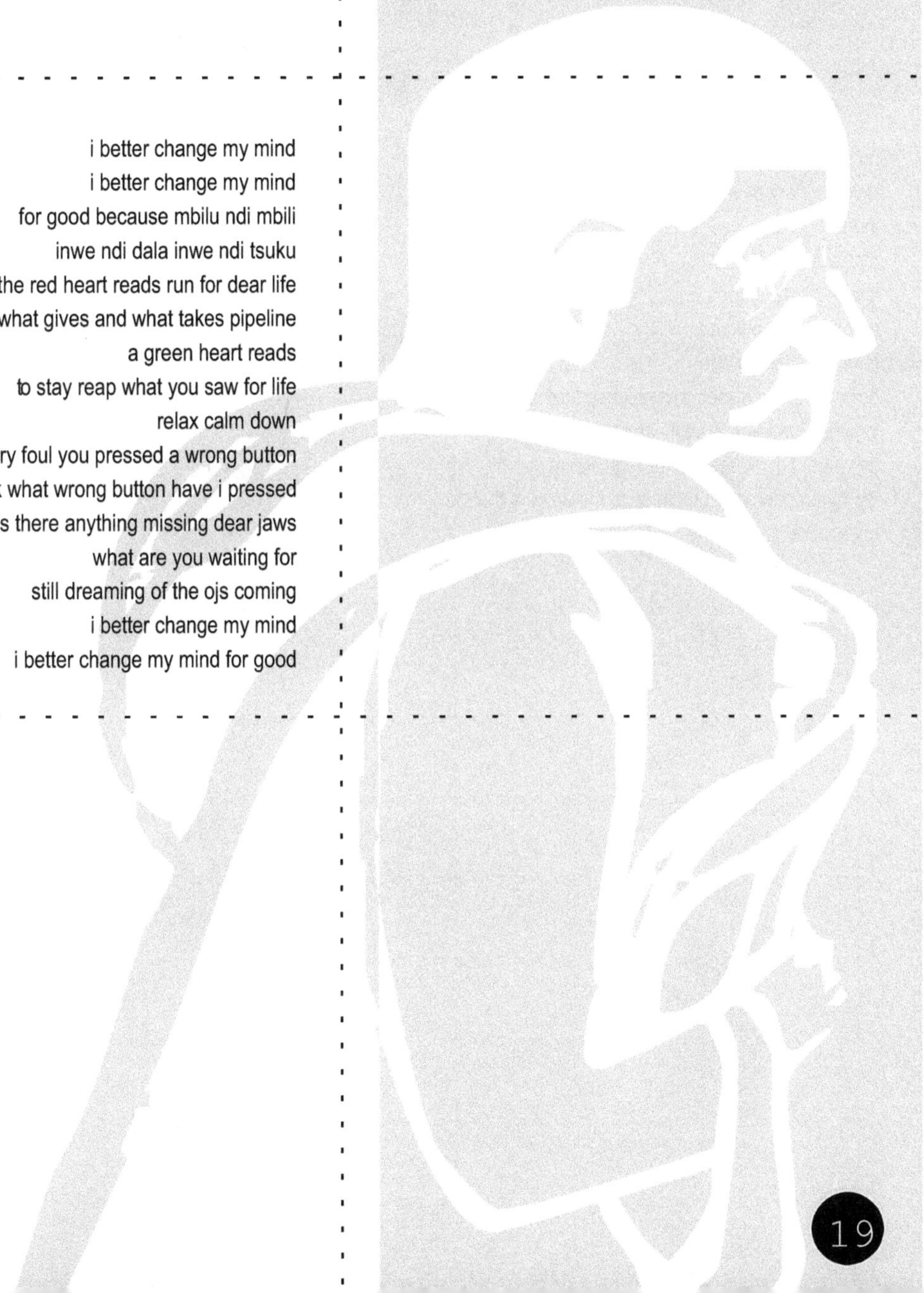

my soul belongs to me

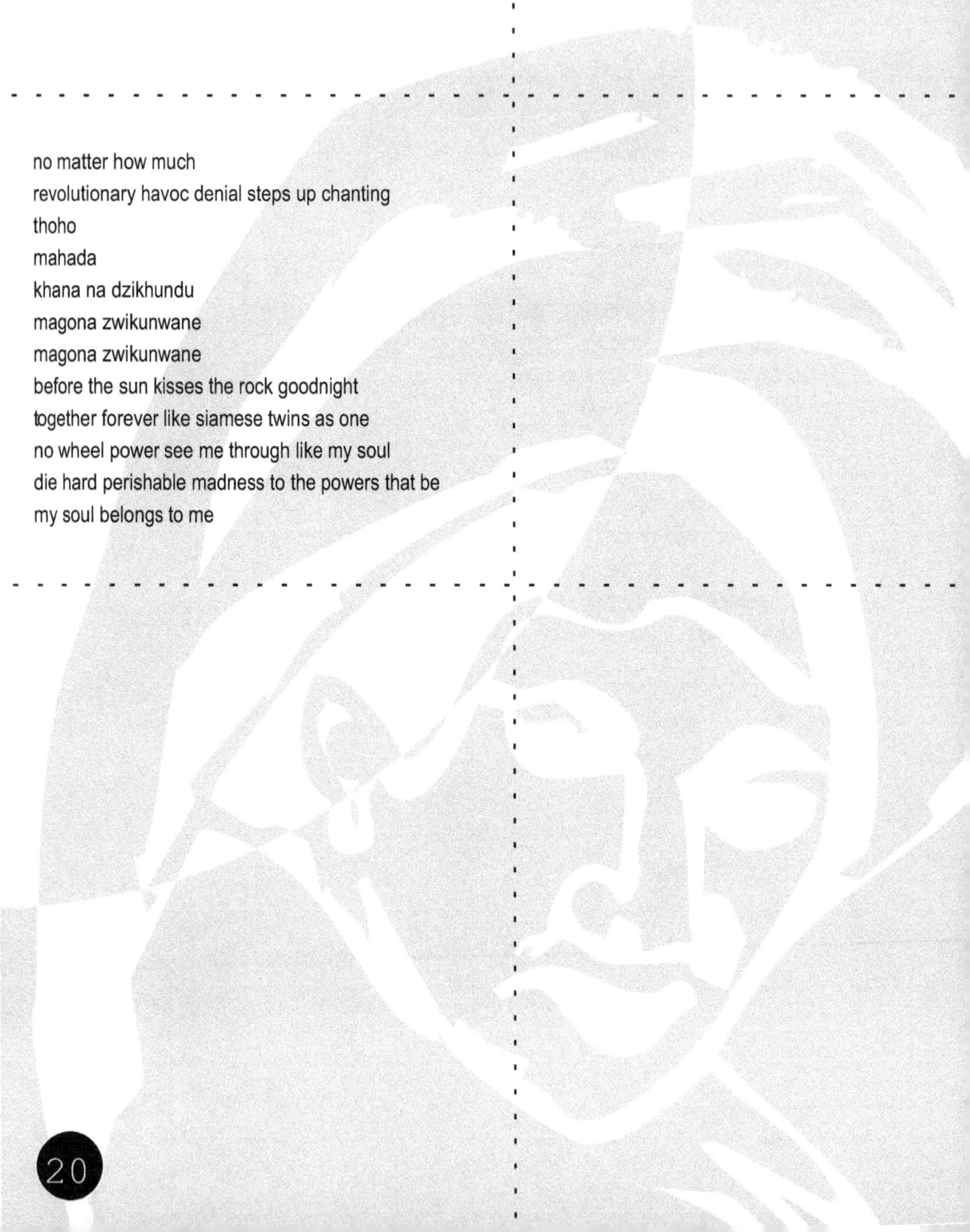

no matter how much
revolutionary havoc denial steps up chanting
thoho
mahada
khana na dzikhundu
magona zwikunwane
magona zwikunwane
before the sun kisses the rock goodnight
together forever like siamese twins as one
no wheel power see me through like my soul
die hard perishable madness to the powers that be
my soul belongs to me

cain cain

cain cain...,
come over
here
cain, cain...,
your brother
muddy
puppet ground
do you remember
kinross mining
disaster
people died
cain, cain...,
come over
here
cain, cain..,
your brother
no benefit
of the doubt
in the battle
of convergence

zone/rwanda carnage
no strings of
countless
figure
to entertain
your butcher
lust
cain, cain...,
come over
here
cain, cain..,
your brother
vaal reef
reef rough
lift of death
naval arse kick
bellyache
cain, cain...,
your brother
vaal reef

dimer
lice under
posh mattress
bayasuza
kumnandi
bazosuza
kubole
cain, cain...,
come over
here
cain, cain...,
your brother
sons en daughters
of the soil
life is hungry
children of asazi
it's cold
outside
come in
from the cold

cain, cain...,
come over
here
cain, cain...,
your brother
remote
sober headword
control
metre size
history
self rewind
war of words
cain, cain...,
come over
here
cain, cain...,
your brother

ngoma kulila side a (i)

ngoma kulila side a (i

ngoma kulila
ngoma kulila is a drum beat thumbs toy
in my heart
whether in sorrow or jubilant mood
ngoma kulila vhana mitanani
tsha ngosha ndi luruli
i want to sing along toys down
follow my heart beat
malogwane
vho matsige vho tuwa na zwiombo
hu bikelwa vhunwanga
vhutsila ri vhona nga mato

i want to sing along the song i really
know brought us from the cold
i want to sing along the song long forgotten
a song for our cultural regeneration
for the youth of tomorrow
ngoma kulila is a drum beat thumbs toy
in my heart
chisa abadakiwe
xolela ababhemi
i want to sing a sing of peace en
reconciliation
repercussion

musanda li edele edelani
i want to sing a song of reawakening
ngoma kulila is a drumbeat thumbs toy
in my heart
ngoma kulila
i want to sing a song of fruitful joy
and prosperity
i want to sing a song of a new dawn
to welcome nuwe gedagte
skomplaas

blomer

blomer

blomer

blomer
blomer madala
ek is ‘n ou taxin terries
binne in die toene
change deurdlana
op en af
blomer madala
blomer jozi
blomer joburg
jakarumba spy vanity logo
big short kota
four five limited tamtasie
ek ken jou haba witty madala
haba stalavisto
niks ou medulla oblongata
blomer
blomer madala
ek spin in die toene ek nou die dag
jy sal never nie skarf kry nie
check lapha site
calaza madala site
ek vang hulle is net dresh
die een.., is ‘n ou mdryseni
die ander een.., is ‘n ou malala
die laste een.., is ‘n ou mavuka
jy moen onthou
skyf is ‘n process
where by cigarettes
passes from the owner to the parasite
blomer
blomer madala

my death
to cesar vallejor

(black stone on a white stone)
i don't know the day to be exact
even though my days are numbered
each time i smoke a chesterfield cigarette
a song wake me up before you go.., go
by george michael could be appropriate
i wish i could die a clean person black out without
even to remember i once lived on earth..,
a team of doctors once woke me up
in a hillbrow hospital
i was brought up to the hospital unknown
all of a sudden in a black out
my memory main switch fell black out in a jeppe street jozi
raindrops drizzling seven thirty pm jumpers
from a fast food fontana inn
when attacked by a morass gang of no particular origin
many a times i dream drowning
which is not a happy experience at all
if you come to think of it
sometimes i dream dying in those severe wars
people trampling all over me awake
like a poppie i wake up dusting off my clothes
to think of it.., it's never a happy experience at all
at the age of eleven
i literally threw myself into an open field public pool
watching my late brother david swimming
i was fascinated gazing at the water which
in turn attracted me to a sudden dive
in which my late brother rescue
saved my life from drowning

photogenic extract

photogenic extract

for sara musundwa moeloa
18 june 1924 - 16 feb 1997

photogenic extract
from a few lines bowl i deliver
eat and drink
its my spiritual soul flesh and blood
a photogenic stripper verse
half moja grand
over cheese spread bite
a frozen moment of the times
enough petrol gadget to fuel
your hungry mental case zosa poppie
i wish i could say i wish i could say
i was also brought up by elderly people mandulo
like the little girl next to me before you
and stop singing me songs
of my sorry sight zabalaza
a combination of my childhood
poverty pain en suffering
vho mme vho mbebela zwone..,
what mothers brought me here on earth for
kha vha do pfa.., listen to that
zwa u dzula mitani ya vhathu..,
to stay in other peoples apartment
kha vha do pfa.., listen to that
ndi tshi-tika matswiya mararu
erecting fire place triangular square
kha vha do pfa.., listen to that
drie voet manyathela shanty sthalala
grannys oppossed to bhayilami walking
sticks of weza weza tuka se dae ek sê

super doom rambo

super doom ramb

super doom rambo
ungu mhlobo wenene
emakhayeni wethu
superdoom rambo
thanyela i cockroach
ne flying insects in our homes
imbizo ya maphela ne mbovane
time and again stray ratas
careless uninvited crawling insects
badbucks of no particular origin
super doom rambo shosholoza
i mosquito rumba dance ngolovane
jive gate crashing in our kitchen unit
heke.., super doom rambo
sibonga wena sgidi bathathe
with your latest uncompromising
deadly blow kwasakemba
now we can sleep peacefully
in our healthy surroundings
leave our foodstuff in the kitchen unit
without fear of amaphela ne mbovane
fly by night come together party breadbin check
sishaya ama get down acid jazz
super doom rambo
skop en skiet en laat hulle sterwe

for takalani musundwa n.p.muila

takalani makhulu ndi tshiulu
ri tamba ri tshi gonya
tshoko tshoko a ili muthu
muthu u liwa nga dzumbulukwane
kha lino shango
zwi tshikonda vhari
ndo rou begwa nda vha muthu
kharali ndi begwe ndi vhe phukha
kudide khotsimunene makandani
dziedzi ngeno ndi mufanadzo
dza maramani
zwitshibala nda vhudza gona
tshirethe murathoni
luvhilo tsetsetse i vhidza u gidima
khorombi mboniseni
luvhambo lwa nndu mutende
bororo la minango mina
sosani fhasi mabasha
dorobonia asi.., kule
mberegeni madodonga
tshanda iya tshanda vhuya
tshoko tshoko steamroller on the move
tshitandani tsitsa nwana u bebe pholisa
keep on moving before the sun set
in the evening we say
malembe mukhathoni lo kovhowa
la kovhela u late mbado
vhusiku ndi dada li a la

damnkos koppie dice

damnkos koppie dice

damnkos koppie dice
kopa dreadful khasa worry in the pocket
children singing
chicken linkin kfc kenturky school laduma
come take a ride with me lingo wise
geen rajah konfyt periperi
spices between my words
damn kos koppie dice
two hearts trace
table queen of spade
tree logo tap roots jack lorry
in the open sky
thorny words pricking tot drie kopstaan gova
crossroads-of-a tempest draadlosie speaker in between

commercial horlosie sun bells bleeding thoughts
dumani kop duik squeezer gova
our cabin cruiser volvo machine deksel tap
in the mobility garage vuma
norokana peach en salt purple boy slippers
mirror tiekie dough bhasela room
horny glue waskers come before dripping wax
willy-nilly special wors dogs lie
pre-primer stove pump hoor fluit
damn kos koppie dice
skhumba touch go rash
lekker krap flower children singing
chicken linkin kfc kentury school laduma

dimmer joe

dimmer joe

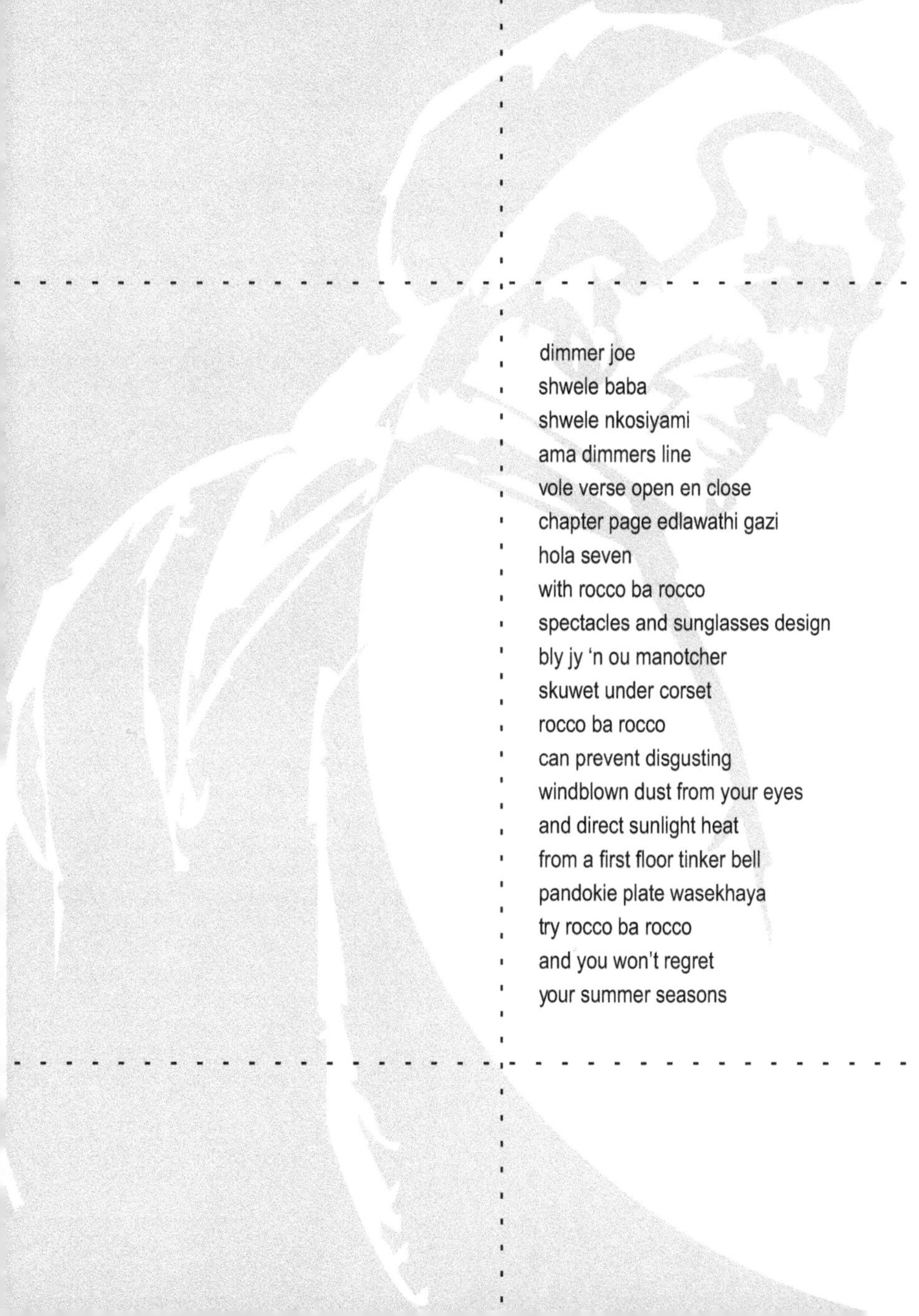

dimmer joe
shwele baba
shwele nkosiyami
ama dimmers line
vole verse open en close
chapter page edlawathi gazi
hola seven
with rocco ba rocco
spectacles and sunglasses design
bly jy 'n ou manotcher
skuwet under corset
rocco ba rocco
can prevent disgusting
windblown dust from your eyes
and direct sunlight heat
from a first floor tinker bell
pandokie plate wasekhaya
try rocco ba rocco
and you won't regret
your summer seasons

salute

tear drops falling like victoria falls
on a chilly winter sun
believe you me mma blonde
jakalasi expecting sympathy
from her swak excuse
when other kids bayile sgele
such a bitter fruit is from a tree
via the roots uya thoasa joe
hakafuzanga phansi lomtwana
as waar mafora mmao seta
education begins at home
she does not have passion for school work
neither here nor there baas jan
six no nine four five kuyafana
mitiro ya balabula masebe

taxi.., 1 side a (i)

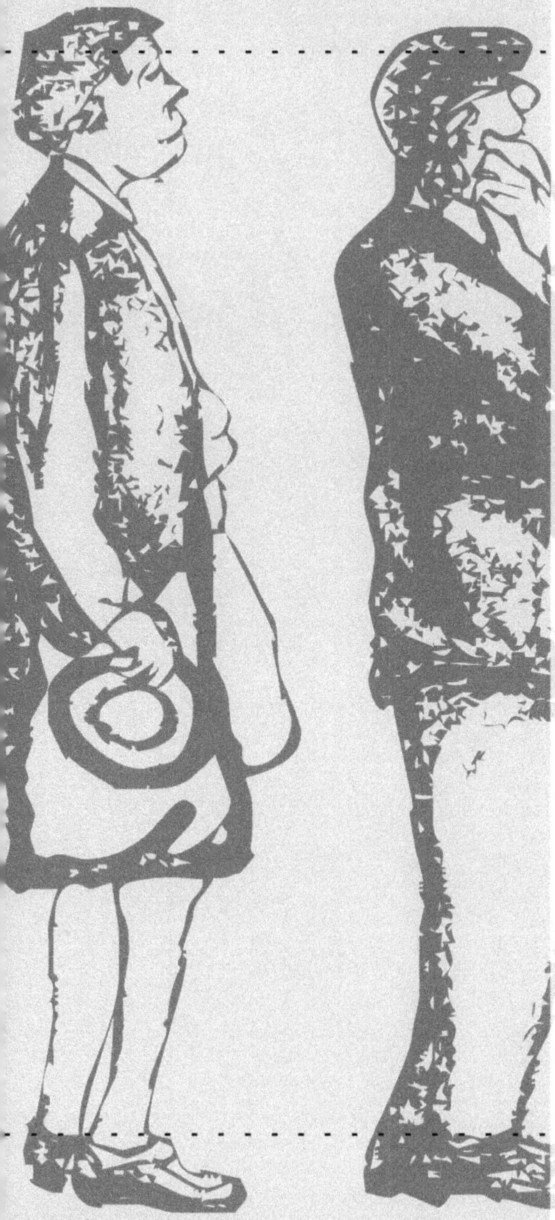

taxi..,
number one office
white city jabavu
bad bucks bid
love bittersweet bite
brief case mower
bobejaan wrench
bloodysucker porterstool
blue bird ribbon shova
rich lorry take five joe man
and zoll – no – fuss
lustig twenty four ringas
pondokie plate
school wydte
mobile darkie capsize
slow down
jackroller hijacker bully
bloody bobejaan wrench
blue bird ribbon
rich lorry dimmer
mum sowetan
soweto city
is a fragmented
piece of land
unholy surrounded
by kak and rubbish
bad bucks bid
love bitter.., sweet bite

dongololo la tsimbi

dongololo la tsimb

dongololo la tsimbi
ba rekisa
malana le mohodo
madombolo
le magwinya
dongololo la tsimbi
ndi la vhurwa
dongololo la tsimbi
li bva vhurwa
a locomotion ready
to swallow a fresh
and early
dressed up platform
to their destination
basopa
platform one
kusuka
amaphepha
kusala
amakhadbox
an iron snake
vomit people
in large numbers
to their destination
ba rekisa
malana le mohodo
madombolo
le magwinya
dongololo la tsimbi
ndi la vhurwa
dongololo la tsimbi
li bva vhurwa

gimba

gimba
tamu tamu intozam
zosa witty zoso gimba
nwana mula malofha mavhisi
thumbuni uyo – nya – hawe
smer-mere old buck dry gin in the pocket
jika majika zosa
tamu tamu intozam
no vhuya na mini nwana-nga
na tshisibe fhedzi
vhurukhu ndi khakhe tshienda ndi sandazi
tennis shoe mateki
phashane daasy more baas halala
hemmbe na badzhi induna touch
maize mealie meal papiersak
gimba zoso umkhulu potato zosa
feed your worms while yours is still alive
morning sunrise shining through my window sill
taxis ferrying people to and from the shilowa express
by the rail tracks dumani gova
jikeleza train on the run
leaving all colours of the rainbow behind
with an empty pot of gold promises across the horizon
like the constant northern star ikhwezi station
alight without.., umngena ndlini my sister
umngena ndlini mamma
umngena ndlini bafoza
umngena ndlini baba
let me feed my worms while yours is still alive
tamu tamu into zam zosa witty zoso gimba
deedum dum dum dummy table
nwana mula malofha mavhisi
thumbuni uyo – nya – hawe

van sidlangozwane

van sidlangozwan

van sidlangozwane
stealing
van sidlangozwi
skuwet under corset
nou skiloog ou koeke moer sê sister
smoke down mzamo
drum ten cook tycoon moleko
dink jy phambili
vole iets wonderlik or kanjani
pump jy nou proper vol
ou koeke moer se sister
shanty dae diesel engine
gum gum guys bubbling gums
wat gat aan service station
draadlosie maker
pump jy mos nou
natural oulik or kanjani
ou topies takal nog al
six mabone page
ballatine chopper skiloog
horolosie bell
seven down skoener
umsila phansi vulavala

madice 1 side a (i)

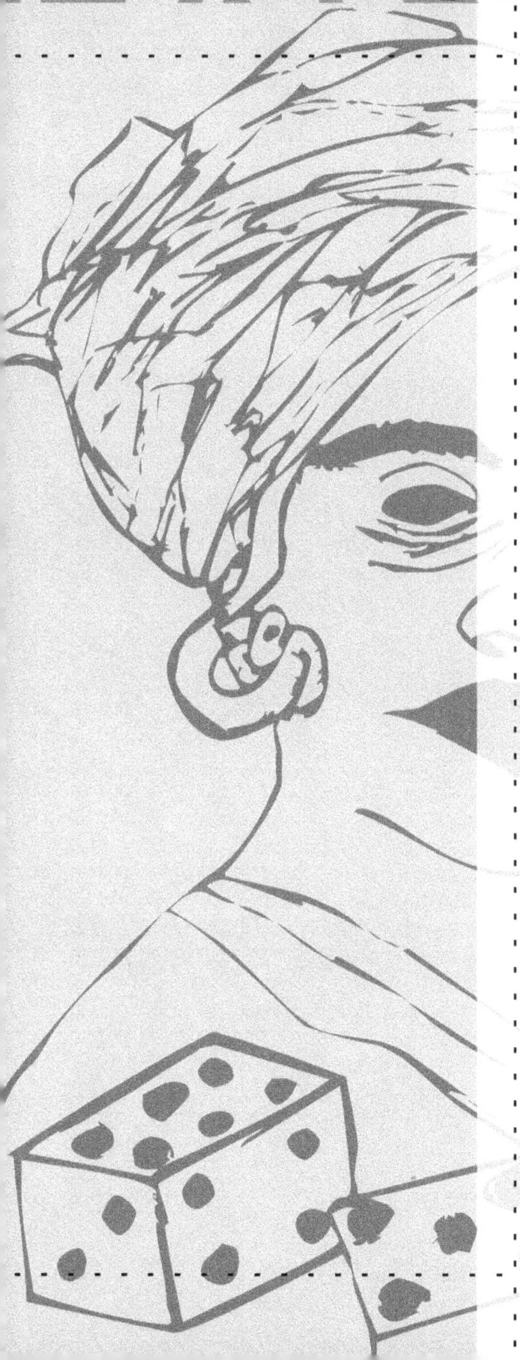

madice
madice rework
double dwesh
two two chances
over quiet storms
three one second
one one school wydte
person to person chaff kop
amehlo ekati
bars two seven
knocksman squadron
eight ou niks
one love service
school bar no drakes
six three four five
six no nine qualify dresh
coward double up
slaat uno one time
take five double slash
labhabha senzeni
kha ndi sekene mutshinyani
kha u lile ludzula back door
ndi maduvha mana
la vhutanu ndi mutshinyalo
vhusiku sala nduni
ha madala khakhu nga li fe
venda ni si luvhe nga mufhetano
mbuya vhuhadzi yo vhuyela
zwi la zwa madekwe
vho muyanalo khotsi a salani
king corn manzhanzha mthombo
mmela ni vha lumelise

madice 1 b side (ii)

1 b side (ii

mazishe
sun shine codesa nonstop
laat hulle brand
anti clock wise
laat hulle verby
clock wise
man to the left
last banduza smaak lekker
like a chicken in the oven
phakhu phokho
popomala durban poison
cockeye sjindane
poke first beshu
spoja wakker
vat en sit teka ufamba
nyangalambuya
bring back latter days
gweva spinza customer
first floor smokers corner
plank fontein pondokie plate
zol no fuss
hoe mean jy nou
vole symbolic these days
mmbo
mmi ndi mmi
mma ndi mma
continue
a round figure rand
sister magwegwe
half crown pringle
evenly divided
in your mind

jamming in my mind

jamming in my mind
to my childhood friend
cude manikiniki.., same style same pattern
as usual as always
thiba izapha
izapha
izapha
izapha thiba
what a marsh mellow jam session in my veins
hell haunted condense milk my mind
ka monwana phezulu.., ting ting tinkling tune
strumming down avenues of my black box brain
decoder gee rajah konfyt pelepele
shisa mbaula
o se ke oa e tswara ka magobe
ntate washa khekhe tshikanda marukhu
behave yourself
dada cable dresser in my skull disco joint
for both eardrums.., zaya molo big fish
where are the small fish
double adopter swivel turn wire
dangling a carrot current flow before my face
that which reminded me of my childhood friends
mpoporia en dingding dancing to the sound of a vithika
troja kuchukuchuku skate mamma shall we pack now
mamma miya chuchu mahala
ziya citheka iishebo tso
thiba izapha
izapha
izapha
izapha thiba

merry my babie

merry
my babie

merry my babie
like whisky
jack d
whisky jack d
whisky jack d
waterfront scheme braai
jobber gate tande face blush
skholana appletiser
spicy salad curry chips drive
merry my babie
like whisky
jack d
whisky jack d
whisky jack d

smart alecs

smart alecs
isicamtho style my sister
luister nou mojanero
jump tyd mmatimba
van gister maobani izolo
ek het jou gawietie
om te sê alles verstaan
sweet no mkatakata nee..,
los dae mooi van ver buddy plaster
jy is half moja bo dae gebou
alles is covered en los chandies
vulavala top shaela slot
haba soek mekaar
nou die laaste
van die one one
finya skuks
ek raak vole-vole
tot daar by die dollie my ousie
skuwet nee
you sing me a song worth singing
smart alecs
is it not good enough that i sing
we – sis – lizah mnta kamaduna
ngizo kuthengela ubhanana
ngina mma pillow case
ngina mma shidi kanye
nombhede wokulala
empondozweni
first floor smokers corner
plank fontein pondokie plate
zol no fuss

mochochonono crazy 1 side a (i)

mochochonono crazy
dry hoek chaff pozi
mochochonono crazy
jigsaw puzzle
capsize milky way
purple light mirror in the mud
how do you operate in the dark
dirty dozen censorship heels
is bova site
doctor feel good ginger cake
fine words butters no pass nips
chopper chopper chappies
mingle mence mence
kulelo verse matwetwe
bo dae hof site
ho che chela moraho
ha se ho balea
ke ho nka stamina
ntate
                    bathi
bambezela tsotsi siya jika
cornerscrash
                                        travelling rugs veranda
stoep no dice
clever tamtasie gebhane
silaphanje
                                        nge mum for man
chaffkop cathawane
mochochonono crazy
jigsaw puzzle
dies milky way

mochochonono crazy 1 b side (ii)

ha bonolo fela
current uno page
haba niks five tense madala site caution
ke sukasihambe msakazi we sizulu
basopa platform one
kusuka ama phepha kusala ama khadbox
isikhathi siya shwabana
wasekhaya
mampara kite
mochochono crazy
jigsaw puzzle
dance milky way
snakes en ladder bhanana kar basela
donsa
barekesa malana le mohodo
madombolo le magwinya
wrong site surveyor madakeni stick in the mud
squealer ry plus minus one problem
vole hebe hebe mushumo haba haba
oxin tailor xashu
ekslaat nou die laste school bar no drakes
tot elke voël in sy nes is or kanjani
of hoe se ek nou die laste madala site caution
welele ebukhosini
sharpover bakhiwa
hola..,
mochochonono crazy
jigsaw puzzle
kite milky way
ha monatifela
hai-kabi

b a f o z a

bafoza

bafoza

bafoza
coca moya steam
coca moya bafoza
kaya ka hina ku na swimange joe
ha sa le do sale great hall dance
nou die laste for the rat race
minkey mouse en mice chipping monkey soul
soos hulle will en dink
when the mother cat is away
cup shape spaza shop teaspoon tips bottle figure
marvellous fanta mix skiloog air spirit wrongs site
madala site puppet string cola punch ndingilizi
vaya slow down goloza hof site
if you see a stopsign calaza
short left en short right mdryseni
haba u turn mjavela twist
coca moya steam
coca moya majozi
from the six nine station rider pee
waya waya spoon down test niks mabuya joe
kaya ka hina ku na swimange na madambi
right across the heart en soul of jozi baba
drive safely papap
dry hoek ndingavela spy
tread your needle with care fafi stall
coca moya steam
coca moya bafoza

dube

vhaya delela vhafana
vhaya delela
niyabasabana
hayi asibasabi siyabafuna
fear go
fear fight
fear go..,
buddy rough dance tshilendele
tshitamba na vhasidzana
hofsite wrong site daas nie plek
for sweet lekkerheid bugger rol hier so nie
bafana bafana
fear go
fair fight
fear go..,
hayi bamba hayi luma bhari
i hate mazondi phangas
goni bhaxaza down
shake hands steady gongsplit
rumble roar in the jungle maseven
fear go
fair fight
fear go..,
los my cherry shaluza saratoga express
magwa dzia nyendelatshilendele
tshitamba na vhasidzana
welele
wele wele wela wela
fear go
fair fight
fear go..,

ek gaan capitol

ek gaan capitol

i am going to the capitol
for dae kroning wil van do
or die indeed
lewe soos danger gevaarlike ingozi
ons is net eenders like siamese twins
ek ke die en danger
cowsing gwavhavha conspiracy gate
geen thatha ama chance bo my
ek gaan capitol
knock knock.., whos there
or wie is daar
jou bra
jou bra who
joe moer

inside of me

inside of me
inside of me joe
the language stream
all assorted jolly eat and be merry
moonlight stars milkshake
bazabaza witness above
inside of me
there is no room for cappuccino
home made brew and beers collide
causing me to vomit
inside of me joe
barekesa malana le mohodo
madombolo le magwinya
oesophagus colour bar print slow down jabs langs aan
inside of me joe
sponge lungs chicken bean bones
flat tubes archer ginger cake spinza oven grey
time tick tock ticks drum turn
fantastic orange heart beat yo yo flex
inside of me
some one is knocking passionately
to no avail
sour kidney structure four five draw
six nine appeal get mchovana
rovers reff hum eh..,
huks vrystaat

dolly

dollyfluit 1(ii) b sid

dollyfluit 1 (ii) b sic

tjovitjo dolly fluit
half moja covered
sharp over is grand hoezit
madala..,
as far as i am concerned
this is my message pin
y2koo.., compliant
tjovitjo tswee..,

venda zulu en tsotsitaal poem
after the myth

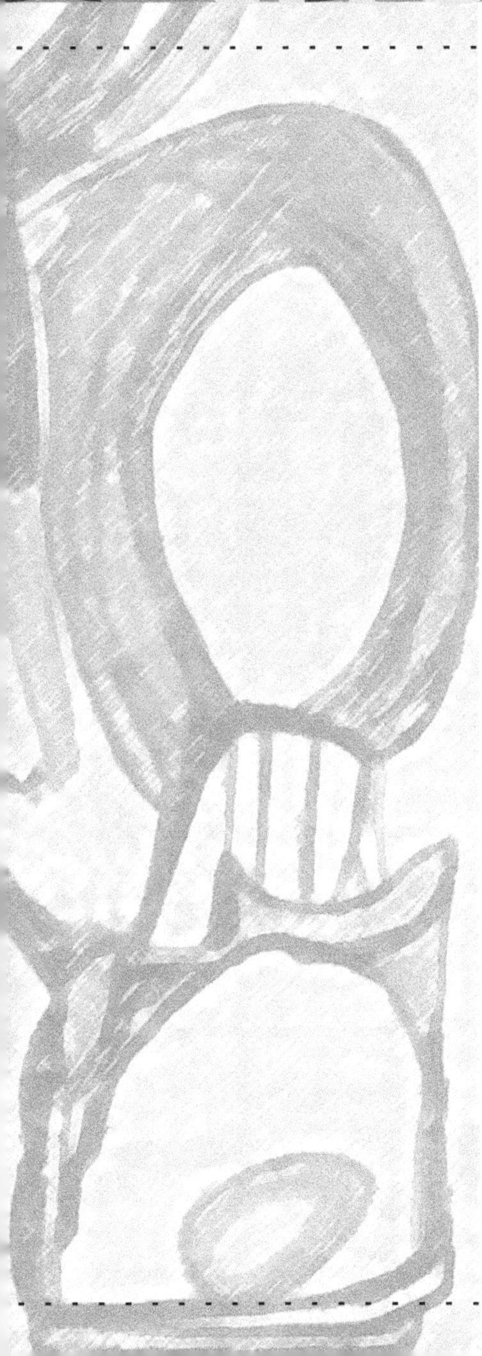

for ndanganeni david muila
4 may 1950 - 17 march 1997

close quote
unquote
(after all is said and done)
after the myth
peter wise ou seun
manotcher
straat mate
peter the hermit slips tonight
vulavala
my royal rod
phashasha
twine two touch golden lay goduka
mdevana
ndanganeni vha loi
vhadzimu vho langana kale
wa ha nyamutsa nga davhi
wa sa tsa nga davhi
ndi vhulombo
thoho ya ndou yo sala muviyoni
mutana wa liwab nga mahunguvhu
across the church yard
in a country's dirty laundry
we buried our differencees
singing hambakahle
lalakahle
emhlabeni
sikhohlela
sigwinye..,
heke!
wakker word
manotcher

kamonyako

kamonyako
kamonyako

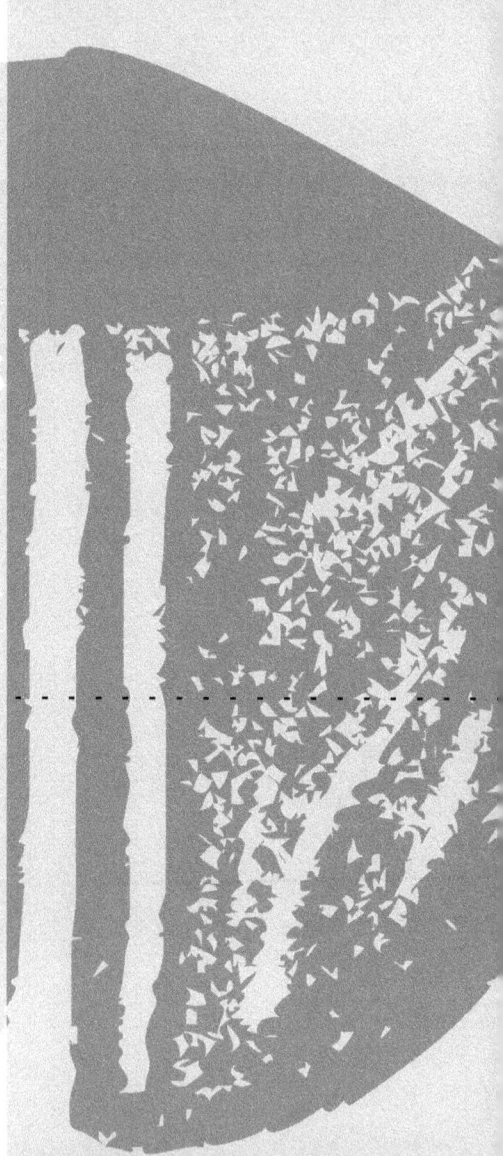

gova..,
kamonyako
dash in your one side step
hip hop sunshine ndingilizi
come on board
walala wasala
bathi kulele okunye
ngabe kubili ngabe kuyavusana
the shilowa express living you behind
a black out entry
red yellow green light beam
gala night caution by
active johnnywalker staap uit nogal
flex on the spot
hastalavista
hesitant masholomba
mish mash marsh mini
dash in..,

botsotsi

a folk song about love

bo tsotsi
ba rata una fela
do; te; la; so
so; la; la; so
do; te..,
ke bale
ba tswere
lovers corner
do; te; la; so
so; la; la; so
do; te;
bo tsotsi
ba rata nna fela
do; te; la; so
so; la; la; so
do; te..,
ke bale
ba jile zamaleke
do; te; la; so
so; la; la; so
do; te..,
ke ba le
bashwela nna fela

mgewu song - a folk song about a naughty fellow

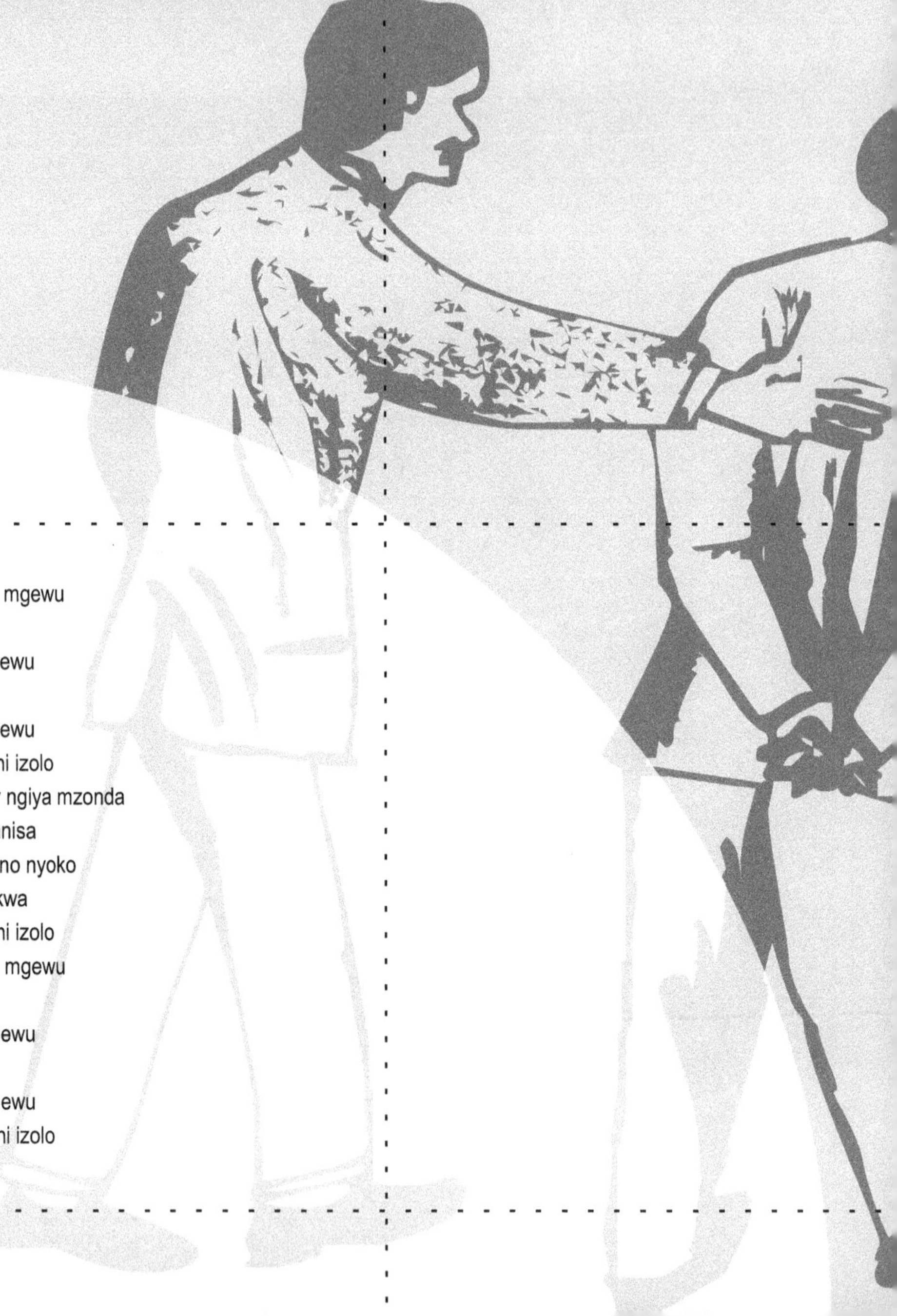

hai we mgewu
iyo..,
we mgewu
iyo..,
we mgewu
ulelephi izolo
u darly ngiya mzonda
u cabanisa
uyihlo no nyoko
hisidakwa
ulelephi izolo
hai we mgewu
iyo..,
we mgewu
iyo..,
we mgewu
ulelephi izolo

my better half

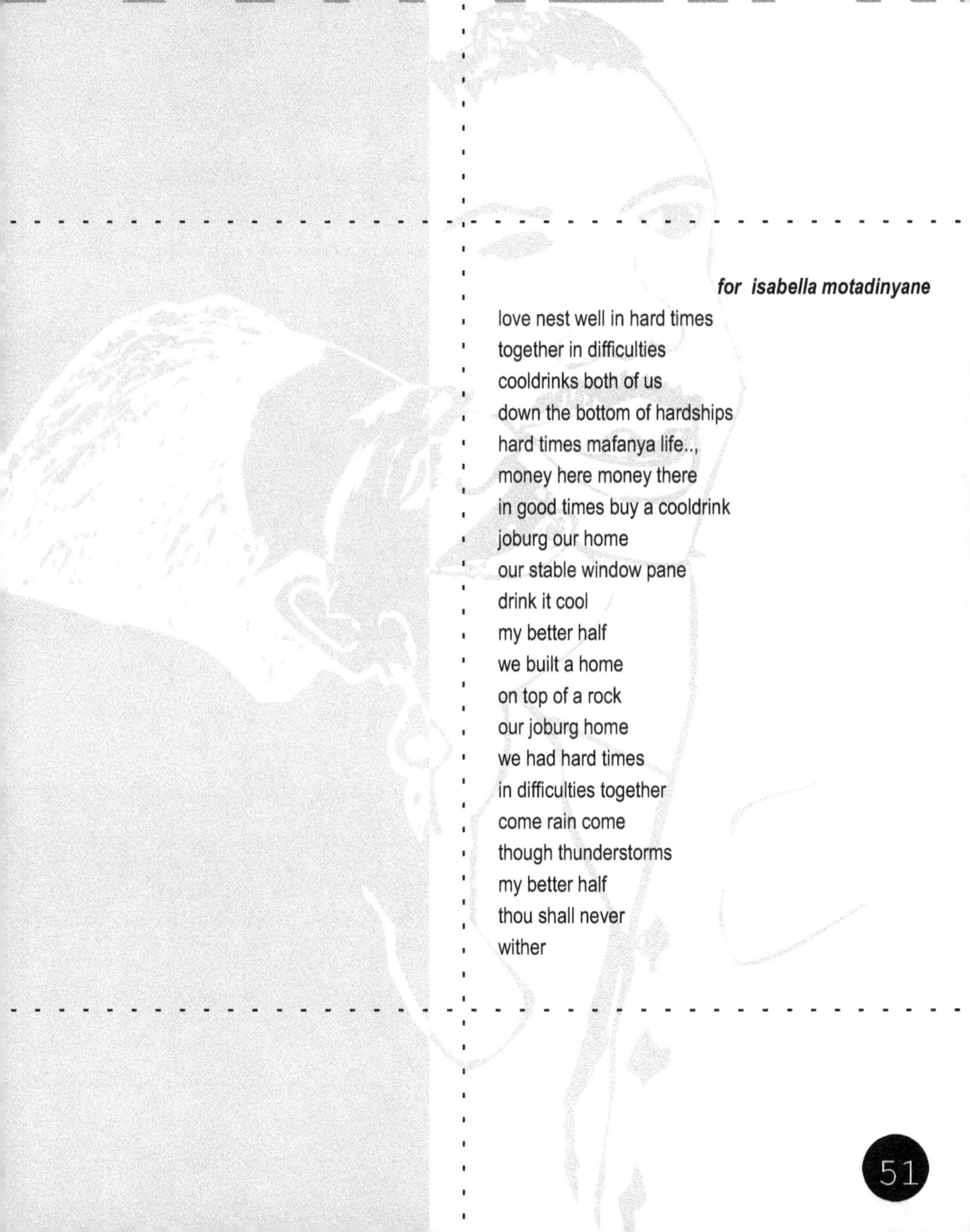

for isabella motadinyane

love nest well in hard times
together in difficulties
cooldrinks both of us
down the bottom of hardships
hard times mafanya life..,
money here money there
in good times buy a cooldrink
joburg our home
our stable window pane
drink it cool
my better half
we built a home
on top of a rock
our joburg home
we had hard times
in difficulties together
come rain come
though thunderstorms
my better half
thou shall never
wither

muyahavho

muyahavho
don't cry
please don't cry
kale kale
ri tshe vhatuku
gone are the days
we were young
vha tshi ri
ndi gukulume
illness tolerance
ri tshi la
muno na madi
water and salt
muyahavho don't cry
please don't cry
half a loaf
of bread
for you to eat

without tea
to drink
take it cool
as it is
much better
please don't cry
early in the morning
you walk
to school
no money for lunch
a little smile
you reserve
release depression
promote a sense
of awareness
don't cry
please don't cry
your teacher

in the classroom
questions
loud and loud
in your head
for the missing
answer
you and me
forget not
the resort
to end the beginning
of our separate world
don't panic
please don't cry
one hungry afternoon
you walk
into the kitchen
you opening doors
of the kitchen unit

the pots are empty
no crumbs inside
everything
is speak and span
nothing
is left for you
don't cry
please don't cry
every dark cloud
has a silver lining
just stomach the pain
as if nothing
worries you
ungakhali akusizi
work all covered
your way out
don't cry
please don't cry

valentine's day

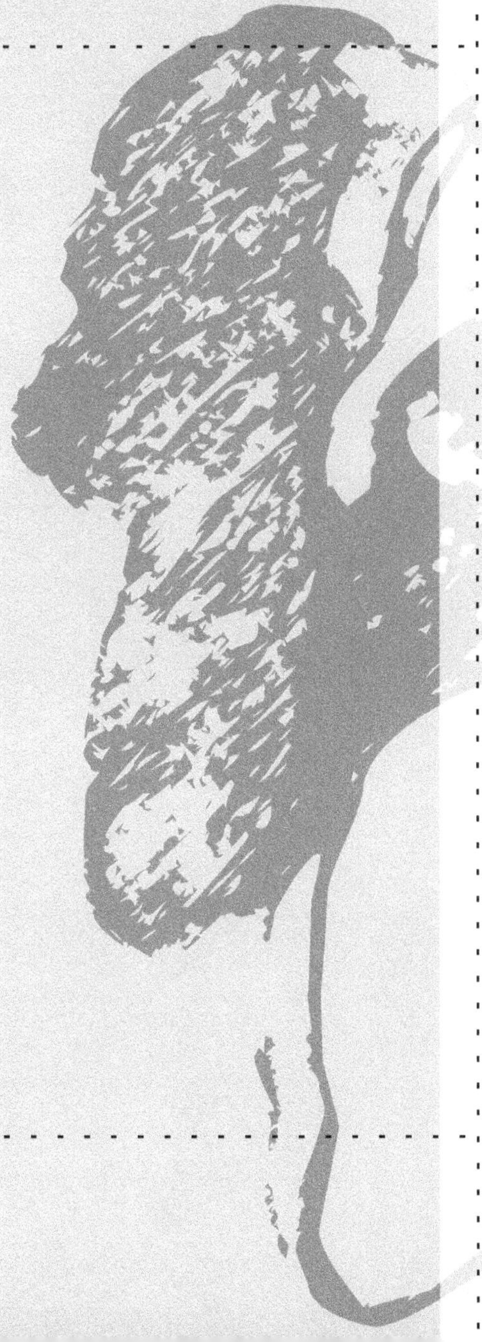

valentine's days
by en bye
wishing you my love
a happy birth day and many
more days to come
mammas tavern dash in
gova get on the bus
washa umkhukhu
over there by the house on fire
waterford kamhlaba
i left you a bone en marrow texture
for the late night content mavusana
staffrider four manyawo dash in gova
setolo ke ntho e nice mdryseni
everybody ride on gova
washa umkhukhu
let's go get on the bus
off to the house on fire
ride on gova let's go see
the zebra crossing kwanyamazane
mina nawe
nne na inwi
ri do ri ndi mbidi
nga u vhona mavhala..,
that is back then in the house on fire
we will eventually say that
this is the zebra crossing
through it's own true colours

secretary bird

secretary bir

unity blazer
broken file sour pan
half crown figure dummy desk
coward ghost masholomba purse
viro lock skiloog
dimmer secretary bird
brokers pan
scrambling eggs
chopper slips no passion
skelm key hardliner rubber neck
in great times
balloon tie
buy your times
like lovers in the air
enjoy the fun
before the fun enjoys you
dimmer jakarumba spy
remember what goes up
surely must come down
birth rite special kite cement
cellular figure guava juice celebrity
dimmer mobile and available
half moja covered
dryhoek chaff pozy jikeleza train
sharp hoezit staffrider
skipper bar block buster score
bella stone dimmer ginger cake bushy
buddy wangu wasekhaya dimmer

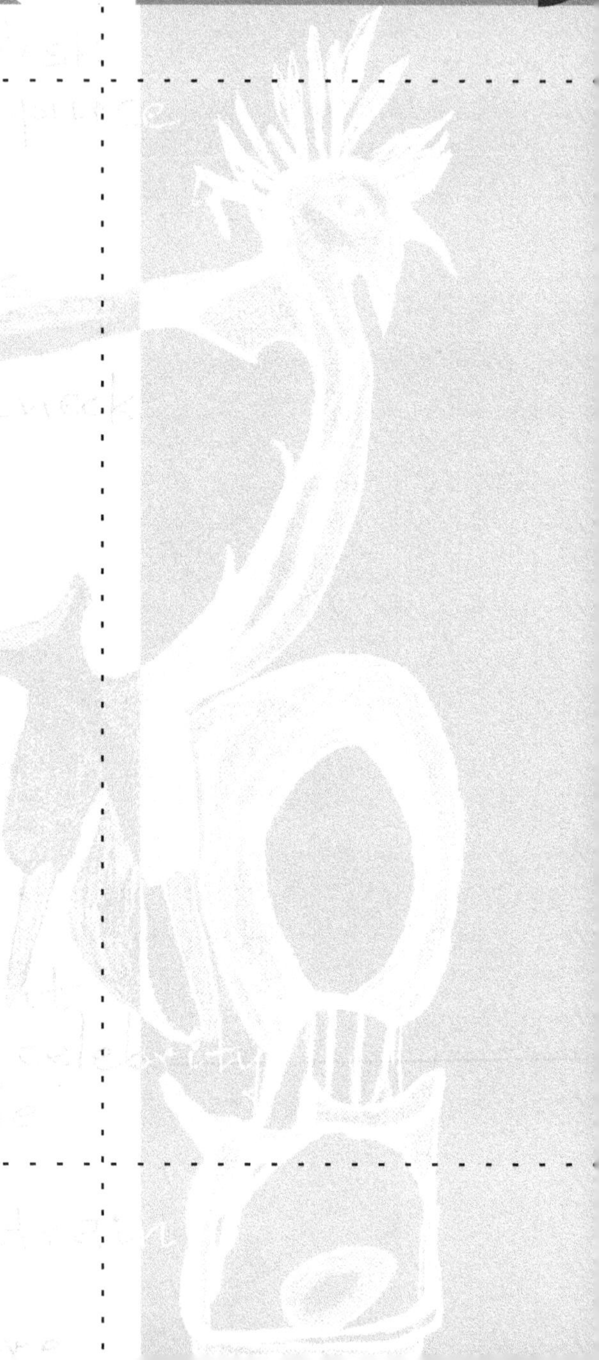

to bra frisco

for bra frisco mukosi muila

side a (i)

bra frisco sacred outcry
ta frisco coffee dascholar
buda buddy frisco
endofaya kusuka amaphepha
kusala amakhad box
kwa ndonga ziya duma
inyama ayi pheli
kuphela amazinyo endoda
buda buddy frisco
van ons duck nie ons phola hier
pf gandakanda hangover stoky hurrah
white pepper poetry fuss food go down crazy
in my system
cockeye gist hurting my consumption capacity
fakazile route draw
bebob german cut ayers
marabi jive mbancanga stokvel halala
for mr fill up the table
en check up the empties
ta frisco coffee dascholar mingle motion
staap uit moen flexible tafula
shiya boy
dexters three piece saxon eyes

for bra frisco mukosi muila

b side (ii)

flour-shem shoe shine tops vulavala
my kroning hero
gazilam throphy jam
buda buddy van my so waar
dascholar gong
no rings en bearings
sharper notch creamora flavoured
of sonder flavour over crony
dascholar companion bras
kopduik one look
hy se voor hulle..,
wonke wonke frisco coffee linothile
liya fudumalisa
kanti lisheshe likuenzele kalula
net 'n oomblik ek sal julle notch
in no time spot on

mamma's tavern

amma's tavern side a (i)

tshele-vhete tow
tshevhere tshevhere
too much about nothing better for the day
lippers cry..,   deurdlana
                boy mgobozi front page
to be continued
i have too many irons
in my welcome dove
a hot chili fire stone
of no electronic ignition plugs
or digital criss cross ragamuffin
microwave hand free network switch blade
                molomo o ja tse chisang
chebere chebere..,
                boy mgobozi le leme
le fiela mabala
a broomstick leaning over
a stop nonsense brickwall of shame
a rubbish bin standing by
for hours on end
                molebe swazini stiff royal mavovo
chebere chebere..,

mamma's tavern b side (ii)

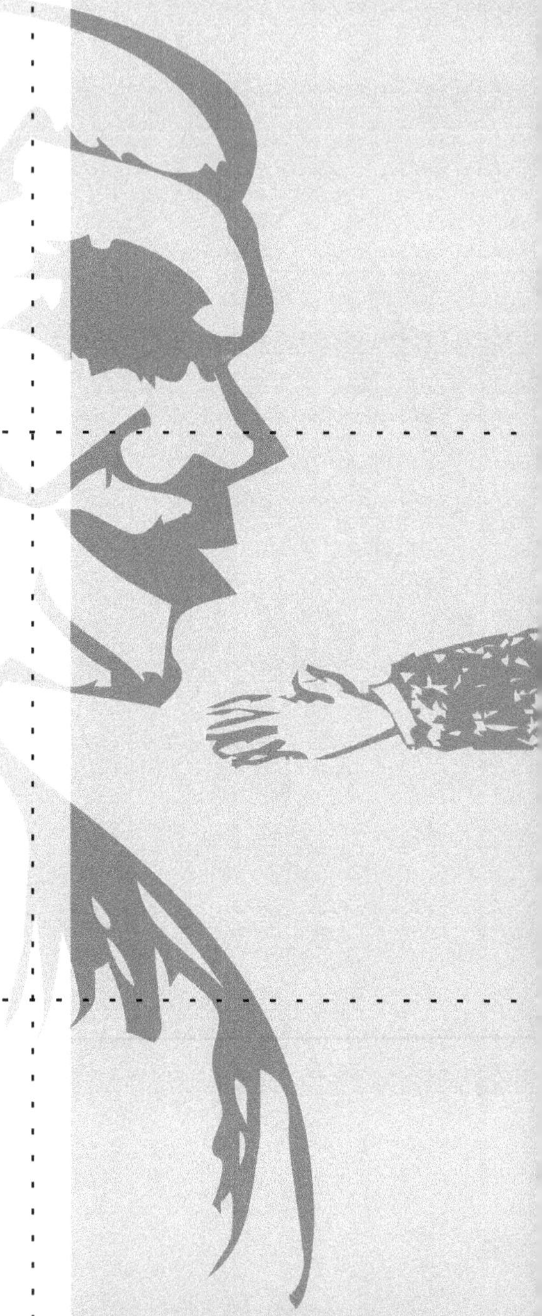

sharing bold en the blended lies
while other steady couch
stil singing a lusaka tune
june nineteen seventy six
nine la come soweto on fire
nineteen seventies bell bottom hippies
around the corner down valley wine brute
chasing honey dew tips
of take five teaspoon sugar in your tea
brothers en sister of love and peace
queens cake giggling
tchebere tchebere too much about
nothing better for the day

samba ndou

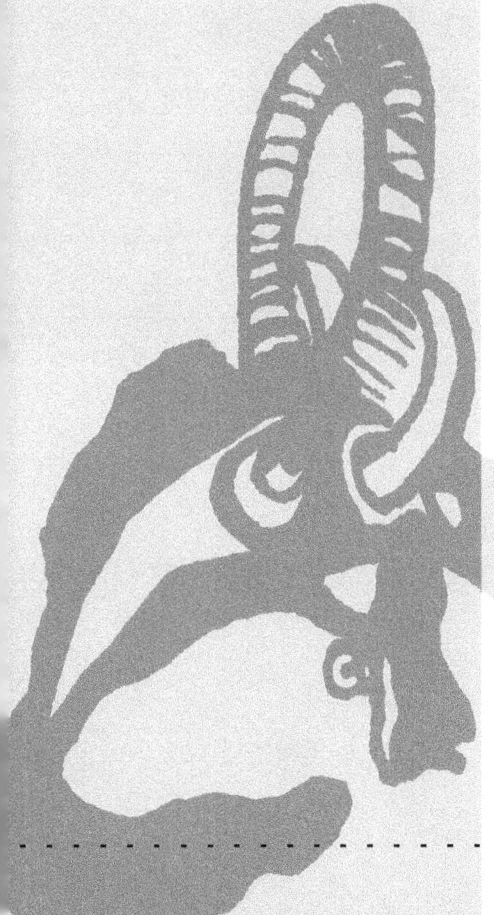

elephants bath
samba ndou
vho shavela ngeno
mushumo khwatha
dzhavhelo bandani
vhashumi mushumo u shavha zwanda
buttershoes on
footprints caterpillar eligible
ebile
dia signer
ebile
dia stamper
shwelebaba
shwelenkosiyami
kanda bongo man
tsha ngosha ndi luruli
if you cannot dance
you better blow your own horn
bongo man
silver sun shine
duluni
vigroece current
salvation spy
papiersak from naledi to jeppe
fish line join the press
sardines bite
saldanha bay love affairs
jikeleza train
vole bashemane ba bapala sigangeni
canada dry music injection

weza weza tuka sê dae

weza weza tuka se da

(from way back days
before the soweto uprisings)
wooden legs three quarter pin krugers sales
trackers in the oven pee
hush puppy ringers breed
wagon wheel fake
a lonely long way
straight buttocks
hasha hasha drinking
amino acid
borderline binder chappies
blue liar chicken murder
bicycle bell papap
hush puppy ringers breed
dirty tyre strippers loo
all over the show
red lips bleach
half dorian troja
stove pipe sunglasses
welcome dove
sugar daddy snacks
plastic smile
hit-and-run spectator
voetsek
oxin tailor garlic puff no dice
toxicated beach tumbler vessel
dove tail sniffer dog
chop chop clear cut
sting wire
dash
hot hit suzuki honda ballad blues
gone astray
freedom of speech tigers don't cry..,

worn-out dirty washing

dirty washing
worn-out dirty washing
grasshopper dash silver bended soul finger
sportless munich machine
ignite your pre-mature
undefined cabin cruiser under the sun
on a dirty washing day
memories flock against
the direction of the wind
jitha buck kofifi dance
turky shoe unmarked
two tone mooi mark
backbone spinner

thina lomhlaba siugezile
with mellow yellow maize
mealie meal stranded
green line troja strictly prohibited
spectacle goggle smoking eyes off
bear bottle tobacco and drug sniffing cocaine
for healthy reasons rizzla belt
phuza face rash
straight en two beers
mail boxer jive
iwisa eating crust
from the pot spectacular
chaff pozzy makoko grap

half barren maize mealie meal pizza
freeze a lot of eat and drink available
children in the playground
no dumping space here
three quarter wear
induna spectator
first gear beshu
change down second-hand
mellow yellow
maize mealie meal
bag t-shirt

khumbani

in a snail
kumbani khumbani
small one ndingavela
golden lay soul finger pressure
malkop caravan
lang one seun jakarumba four five
base two staffrider
ngo lovane
hill extension gaatsak
pilikie vonkel toe sluit
wat lag jy
jan van riebeeck
dink jy gaat sak
ek is ou father chrismass
buck short botsotso
skop en skiet jan pampoene
spare twine two touch
mbazo slash
soweto buck short garage
grand covered spaza workshop
rema jy nou gaat sak
bless kop masana rain
hoe lyk jy nou dae
spanner kop brakate skaap
twine two touch
double slash
labhabha take five
hayani heke..,

in no time side a (i)

in no time

spot on
infidelity
security injection
buy and sell
small small
in any way
you ought
to be
over quive
current by now
meet werksman
vho maita zwitoma
tshinyakaila vhutsila ndi vhutoko..,
create friendship
in any way
in no time
spot on
grab malaza
a piece job
madala site
deadly ghost
weave
inner my bones
down the marrow
to the core
catch my tail
worn out
day in
day out

in no time b side (ii

in no time

hand out
dreadlocks
phashasha
in no time
spot on
asimuboni ebafazini
simubona emadodeni
asimuboni emadodeni
simbona ebafazini
rascal starring
in your eyes
heartcahe
attack
handout
dreadlocks
phashasha
in no time
spot on
when we cry
work for all
singing justice
mulalo
over the land
inner bubbling
peptalks
madzingandevhe
fresh air quiver
you play me
black mapatile
banya ba ipatile
hide and seek game

in no time

›ward flops
yzermadala site
:op dry oorklappies
ıas boy boss
‹trastrongenzyme
ıarp one look
ıeep
ıashaha
crocodile smile
ıoke down mozamo
ır terms never alter
ıu give us
break
no time
ıot on
e sinking
ıtirely from a hand
the mouth
ıales by
ıd large
assorted mess
ake down
a climb
ıergency siren alight
ısist car loggerhead
ısualty desert
ıbulance flashlight
ıck spinning

in no time d side (iv)

hospital stain
garinja wangu
tshiguluzwana
matopeni
u dzula
hu naka
u sea
buddysoul
in particular
an island
unholy surrounded
in no time
spot on
a helicopter pest
blue dock
standing jacket on
in a world
trade centre
mix vegetable
green flies
third force
foul acid rattex
vole yellow
pandemonium
graph choken throat

in no time e side (v)

bitterness never smoke
nwananga o taha
hundred thousand
dowry
u vhala
ndi muila
inyongo ringas
spitting words
undilutable bile
international
minister
of foreign affairs
emzansi africa is
a world
in one country
indeed
you name it
pungent chaff
in no time
spot on

bekkersdal marathon 1 side a (i)

to h.c.bosman

bushveld bekkersdal marathon affairs its our own
europe going for a nonstop marathon dancing record
bushveld bekkersdal shesha dominee welthagen in a
lonely long distressing trance similar to
abafana basezola fits inner injury steyns
post office rich lorry spoondown test waya waya
a naude loud speaker marathon affairs
soos hulle is van both die selde
groot marico se towenaar
deacons taking turns in tiptoe visit to
konsistorie for twirls of the nagmaal wine
the organist medicine indicator twirls nogmaal
in a hidden lonely long black bottle manel
for all day long sustainable piano energy
tp break a monotone sequence
of a verse follow verse
pouse succeed pouse
unlike papist kind of singing
a presbyterian spooky singing of psalm 119
with hundred en seventysix verses
three burly native convicts in red stripes jerseys
overtake the handle from koster claasen and the
assistant verger singing as usual
bekkersdal ikhaya lethu
esili.., thandayo..,
all three burly native convicts in red stripes jerseys
and in the bakhathla tongue threatening mutiny amen
sounding like less than a score of voices hoarse with
singing psalm 119 with hundred en seventysix verses
divided into sets of eight verses.

1 b side (ii)

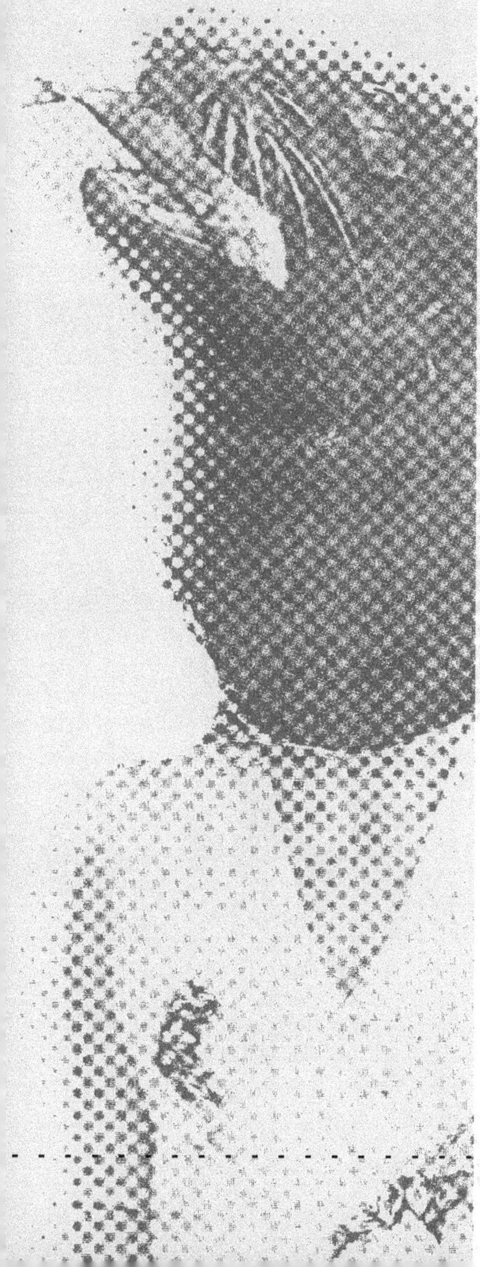

tussen each ending with the word pouse
en jy moet nou weer van die begin af
sing psalm 119 tot piet kom
repeating over and over again
each time dominee welthagen is driven under
abafana basezola fits attack
with a rigid upright body frame
and a head forward flip flop
bekkersal marathon at naude nonstop
spoon down test wayawaya niks mabuya joe
before going into a trance all over again
he would announce a hymn for the evening
repetition over and over again
tot piet kom is waar
dominee welthagen riding in the mail of
abafana basezola fits nonstop waya waya
bushveld bekkersdal marathon affairs
all three burly native convicts in red stripes jerseys
and in the bakhatla tongue threatening mutiny amen
singing as usual
bekkersdal ikhaya lethu..,
bekkersdal ikhaya lethu
esili.., thandayo..,

extract from a muvenda journal seventy si

from a muvenda journa

thaii (riddles) a maroon fob above
the mountains of luonde..,
that's a sun bleksem gova
dash in en face dae waaruit bakhiwa
on that fly page wangu
of the so called poetry book gova..,
thaii.., gambana tsuku thavhani ya luonde..,
that's a sun bleksem gova come on board
dash in en face dae reality gazilam
gova borg zwakala nine nine
is so maar net om te se
face dae reality sonder oogklapies lapha site wasekhaya
of hoe se ek
nou die laaste madala site caution
gova is a language movement
behind a black moses bakhiwa
yours sincerely

wangu ike muila

selected translations

wangu dear ike

my dear ike

my dear ike
where and how are you
now this time of the evening humours town
there is no lover nearby for dice
clever piggish fellow spy
there is no time in humours town
how do you figure this tsar
where are my love letters
i keep on sending you to no avail
you are ignorant ike..,
i believe you believe

that we all believe you are
what you write about
baby you are a tsotsi
in a tsotsistaal skin my love
where did we go wrong
in those sweet moments of love
covered under a blanket
humours town hanging on the edge of eternity
hang on tsotsi we are taking a turn
cornerscrash travelling rugs veranda stoop no dice
my word listen to that

my man is madly in love witty wise
i mean in love with the so called tsotsitaal
a home lingo mix buddy
kindly do return my love regards
in a half liberated witty lingo i say
or how do i say now lately this thoughtful
sight caution
so, so, well, well..,
yours sincere love
moody style
x love in disarray

buddy scamtho

lingo mix buddy

lingo mix buddy
first and fore most i accept and thank you
for your invitation
with my most humble beginnings
lingo mix buddy jam
child of mother smoke
carry on location movie style
hold on tight my mothers child
nail hammer chisel follow up driver
dish dash home let alone hot stolen property this site
frightful work its hot in south africa bullish.., coward
i am into creative writing as a poet artist performer
my naratives oral mix is in eleven
languages spoken in south africa
by and bye trapped in one poem
the so called tsotsitaal lingo mix alive
and kicking sense of humour in you and me
mixing of languages into a witty lingo
a language of identity
a language of an ordinary person in the street
a language of unity in diversity

happiness in the heart, is a child
chu chu baby, is a child
talk talk baby, is a child
cry cry baby, is a child
ah, ah, baby, is a child
oh, oh, baby, is a child

a song happiness in the heart, is a folk song
by the malende dance culture which says what brings
happiness to the heart is a child..,
in this instance
the ultimate child
in my case
is lingo mix buddy

bottle kop shova

bottle neck pusher

bottle neck pusher
locust out fit burst
disturbing attraction meet the eye
wholesaler rap strictly casual dakota whistle
snuff box sandals tennis shoe shine khaki
muddy plastic hot hit rubber shoe smelling socks
harrow scent forbidden fox are you aware pepe
teachers rope file reading goggle at school
copy dungarees goal keepers fence
its happening good time at seven for lifes place
try spy food glutton captain
on the other side they are roasting
bottle neck pusher
sausage and tea bone steak fry
only to find that greedy eater just throw
and swallow hot meat
thoughtful site stealer get real
forgery at its best what's going on
party line plastic figure penny penny guy foxy
children case open and close chapter verse
of throw in and throw away mindless taste
come on board burst.., morning after party bells
bottle neck pusher
three artificial body parts
false teeth couple gimmicks inside bathroom toilet
digging an anglo sex language poem
back ground bottle neck pusher camera roll
action...

jack in a bootleg

jack in a bootleg

durban line
telephone director tf
they are smoking bb best blend zol
half a jack nip
sweet gulp brown sugar
just throw in dry yeast there about
spoon down test pass over home brew
hold me tight and let me move calabash wise
sandy hatch dirty shoes corner jive
shake shake drop by drop wild morula fruit tree song
liquor over here seven
hello mothers near the wild red fruit tree
fountain square
canary time keeper goalie of the wall
cool mate friend be aware
s.a brewery
three foot face quarter share
clean and green like
african dustbin caring a tree of liberty
that waters blood
of the martyr

this poem ...,

this poem ..,

this poem..,
is an extension of love index
blue mass trap
logger dancer
in between

- venus and mars
- calabash archer stalk me
- inside out of an imaginary planet
- calabash logger dancer
- a bundle pot scraper spinach fence
- junior buck short
- love index of discomfort
- eloff street candy collar
- rebels
- corner market and nugget
- cake tale story turn around both site
- washing brake coffee bar
- gauteng city lights
- commissioner benrose
- ellispark calibres
- pullout
- referee spy
- only to find dry skin in touch salvation spy
- dry skin grace vaseline
- blue seal petroleum jelly stop station
- service touch line
- slander water proof
- dramatic order disorder
- in disguise
- wardrobe blinkers
- munching
- exclusive blue mass

i stare in wonder

i stare in wonder
stockings kilo meter bum jive grand
party house management pulling out
stinking boots and knicker bondage of country
socks enticed by naked future feminique
sinking no strings attached
to love fencing spearhead tumbler
within a bottomless whore shacks
unknown rough and ugly
ginger four feet pause a threat
to innocent heart broken container
i stare in wonder
jack roller without a heart driven fear
on that dairy fortress children of who knows what copy
only to find that huks free state get moving
spoon down test
the silver cup is broken
if you see a stop sign in this area
pusher take no u turn
take a glance syndicate then
short left or short right
all the way without turning back joe
my friend do you understand properly
very well
you hit me dizzy wrong site
with shocking work of lights on and off jive
deedum dum dum
dummy table
i stare in wonder
them sluggish fat cow smoking a zol
on that joint outside the back yard wood
resembling them earring bulls without horns
sharing a blade in the ghetto jol

1 b side (ii)

i stare in wonder

a three foot face dose of marijuana
monkey do smoking a home made pipe
like a bottle neck pusher
i stare in wonder
looking at the sacred tree camp
nearby makonde mountain range
when it dawned in my mind
that a mother insectivorous plant does exist
which preys on anything alive even human beings
who dare go nearby the tree
no wonder it is believed
you could only escape the sacred tree catch
if and only if you go nearby naked to the tree
i stare in wonder
failing to escape the loudness in my mind
my in law mulamu and i turned to listen
with all that funny feeling jogging in my mind
to bob marley's reggae music in a car
music with the philosophy of generations yet
to come by and ponder about war in the middle
east of nation war against nation
i stare in wonder still
cruising all over the mutale region
surrounded by the makonde mountain range
malondi and takalani in the back seat of a car
singing a venda version
on one of bob marley's songs
indeed ..,
those who are weak and lazy are no where

pretty woman man ..,

pretty woman man ..,

pretty woman – man or man – woman
either way in the township is the same
that is not so bad to guarantee chesterfield
easy samson strip strong rider overall vest
leather jacket jones and mafia shoes
kid lesbian bride groom pretty well
what a gay guy lesbian stem tide
to the powers that be
on a syndicate foxy line
of animal offal business dealer coast
dish take eye balls animal brains testicle
tongue livers hand to the traditional healers
pretty well cheer up healers
pretending a dynamics portion for life

private human body part mystery chemistry wise
in the traditional healers pretty get well industry
the marriage initiation failer to man woman
from macheke street eye witnesses
a buyer who ate free gifts returning the goods
a gay guy lesbian free bioscope parade
white wedding ululation from street corner to corner
a sudden doorway steps fortune favour fools
tv scoop journalist gunning for the news break
at a mofolo village back yard house in soweto
a law suit pull triggers tomato sauce ellisa giggling
pretty oil defrauding sabc tv people for deformation of character
who me ..,
you see me and take for granted you know me

ngoma kulila

drum beat cry

drum beat cry
drum beat cry is a drum beat thumbs toy
in my heart
whether in sorrow or jubilant mood
drum beat cry children on your backs
for the dancer is dust
i want to sing along toys down
follow my heart beat
ringleader
the drummer is gone with the drumsticks
we cook or prepare a traditional healer
for art we look or study with our eyes
i want to sing along the song i really
know brought us from the cold
i want to sing along the song long forgotten
a song for our cultural regeneration
for the youth of tomorrow
drum beat cry is a drum beat thumbs toy
in my heart
burn drunkers
reward smokers
i want to sing a song of peace and
reconciliation
repercussion
your highness kingdom let sleeping dogs lie
i want to sing a song of reawakening
drum beat cry is a drumbeat thumbs toy
in my heart
drum beat cry
i want to sing a song of fruitful joy
and prosperity
i want to sing a song of a new dawn
to welcome new mind location

hang around

blomer

hang around
hang around buddy of mine
i am an old texas town
inside my toes
changing door to door
up and down
hang around buddy of mine
hang around jozi
hang around city johannesburg
vanity logo foolish spy
big short quarter
four five limited witty case
i know you have no wits buddy of mine
no bye bye
nothing like an old medulla oblongata
hang around
hang around buddy of mine
i spin inside my toes these days
you will never receive pass me a smoke
check this place
peep cautiously this place
i believe these are three only
this one is for while away time
the other one for when is time to sleep
the last one for when you wake up
you should bear in mind
pass me a smoke is a process
whereby cigarette passes
from the owner to the parasite
hang around
hang around buddy of mine

super doom rambo

super doom rambo

super doom rambo
you are a friend indeed
and also in need at our homes
super doom rambo
sweep all cockroaches
and flying insects in our homes
a come together party of cockroaches
and crawling insects
time and again stray as they please
careless uninvited crawling insects in our homes
bad bucks of no particular origin
super doom rambo move out
the mosquito rumba dance cart
jive gate crashing in our kitchen unit
that's it.., super doom rambo
we thank you bulldozer over taker
with your latest uncompromising
deadly blow jive axe
now we can sleep peacefully in our healthy surroundings
leave our foodstuff in the kitchen unit
without fear of cockroaches and crawling insects
fly by night come together party breadbin check
we play them get down acid jazz
super doom rambo
shoot kick and let them die

for

takalani musundwa n.p.muila

for takalani

be happy that granny is like an anthill
where we play around climbing up and down
frightful hisses clocking clicks means
no harm to anyone
what victimises a person is that
which suddenly strikes
in this land when faced with problems
they say why on earth was i born to be a man
i wish i was born an animal
my fathers younger brother pondokkie in limbo
problems on the other hand
is craziness of dying in silence
with a lot of undesirable stories to tell
failing to do so
i tell my stories to the knee
dragging hills on a steep slope
speed calls for a run
bad company door way show me a royal palace
a rondavel house with four entrances and exit
mr nobody town at bay down with beer hall taverns
disorientation in me is at work
hand over go hand over come
steamroller locomotion train on the move
park woods stationary logs bring down the child
up lift the police on your back
keep on moving before the sunset
a rock fall stone the sun
tools down put away the axe
in the evening we say is a harmful ghost
in the dark

damnkos koppie dice

damn cost cuppa dice

damn cost cuppa dice
copy dreadful crawling worry in the pocket
children singing
chicken linkin kfc kenturky school strike
come take a ride with me language wise
no rajah jam peri peri
spices between my words
damn cost cuppa dice
two hearts trace
table queen of spade
tree logo tap roots jack lorry
in the open sky
thorny words pricking until triangular hot head come on board
crossroads-of-a tempest radio speaker in between

commercial sun clock bells bleeding thoughts
head plunge squeezer last coach come on board
our cabin cruiser volvo machine cover tap
in the mobility garage rev
mini dress peach and salt purple boy slippers
mirror tickey dough hand over room
horny glue candle come before dripping wax
willy-nilly special sausage dogs lie
pre-primer stove pump hear whistle
damn cost cuppa dice
skin touch go rash
sweet scratching flower children singing
chicken linkin kfc kenturky school strike

dimmer joe

dimmer joe

dimmer joe
over you father
over you my lord
them dimmers line
full of verse open and close
chapter page home my blood
hallo seven
with rocco ba rocco
spectacles and sunglasses design
you stay the same wiser
covered under the blanket
rocco ba rocco
can prevent disgusting
windblown dust from your eyes
and direct sunlight heat
from a first floor
tinkerbell
hovel plate home buddy
try rocco ba rocco
and you won't regret
your summer seasons

dongololo la tsimbi

an iron centipede

an iron centipede
they are selling
tripes meat
dumplings
and fat cakes
an iron centipede
is from the south
a locomotion ready
to swallow a fresh
and early
dressed up platform
to their destination
watch out
platform one
out flies papers
cardboard boxes
remains behind
an iron snake
vomits people
in large number
to their destination
they are selling
tripes meat
dumblings
and fat cakes
an iron centipede
of the south
an iron centipede
from the south

greedy eater

gimba

greedy eater
envy me with my own eat and drink
eat witty food greedy eater
a child who eats raw blood
stomach pains shit his or her own way
smirnof old buck dry gin in the pocket
turn around and eat
envy me with my own eat and drink
what have you brought home my child
i brought in a soap only
a khaki trousers canvas shoes
tennis shoe rubber shoes sandals
there he goes good morning sir halala
a shirt and a jacket made out of induna touch
maize mealie meal bags
greedy eater your are great potatoe eat
feed your worms while yours is still alive
morning sunrise shining through my window sill
taxis ferrying people to and from the shilowa express
by the rail tracks last coach come on board
merry go round train on the run
leaving all colours of the rainbow behind
with a pot of gold promises across the horizon
like the constant northen star ikhwezi station
alight without.., anything to come home with my sister
anything to come home with mamma
anything to come home with my brother
anything to come home with my father
let me feed my worms while yours is still alive
envy me with my own eat and drink eat witty food greedy eater
deedum dum dum dummy table
a child who eats raw blood..,
stomach pains shit his or her on way

van sidlangozwane (meaning nepotism)

eating in terms of relationship
stealing
eating in terms of a forefinger
covered under corset
now cockeye old cake nut sister
smoke down attempts
drum ten cook tycoon temptation
you think ahead of you
full of wonderful things or what
pump you now properly full
old cake nut sister
let alone that diesel engine
gum gum guys bubbling gums
what's going on service station
radio maker
pump you indeed
now natural wonderful or what
grannys hit once more still
six lights page
ballatine chopper cork eye
time ticks
seven down shoe
tails down open and close

the dice 1 side a (i)

the dice
the dice rework
double twice
two two chances
over quiet storms
three one second
one one school wide
person to person take a cover
cats eye
burst two seven
knocks man squadron
eight over nothing
one love service
school bar no drakes
six three four five
six no nine qualify dresh
coward double up
strike one once for all
take five double slash
clap what have we done
innocent let me run away
carry on cry happiness back door
is only four days
on the fifth day tables turn around
goodbye luminous dark in the house
divide and rule perish
let peace rein venda and worship peacefully
a lady returns home from marriage
tired of last night bedroom politics
wandering father always on the route see you..,
kingcorn home brew sorghum beer
thanks for going pass my greetings

madice

the dice 1 b side (ii)

let it burn
sunshine codesa nonstop
let it burn
anti clockwise
let it pass over
clockwise man to the left
last bench taste so good
like a chicken in the oven
a crackers pull and brake down sound
popomala durban poison slow down
corkeye herb
first run poke
liveliness is the stub
take bind and passover
godess of love
bring back latter days
beer customer buy
first floor smokers corner
plank fountain hovel plate
zoll no fuss
what do you mean now
fully symbolic these days
mmbo.., is a gesture of giving
giving is giving
mothers are mothers
continue
a round figure rand
sister bowlegs
half crown pringle
evenly divided
in your mind

jamming in my mind

jamming in my mind
to my childhood friend
trouble torn tattered head on a challenger
like a hen.., same style same pattern
as usual as always
backoff comeover
comeover
comeover
comeover backoff
what a marsh mellow jam session in my veins
hell haunted condense milk my mind
with a four finger on top of the ting ting tinkling tune
strumming down avenues of my black box brain
decoder gee rajah jam spicy chillis
fire brazier burn don't touch yourself with food
soiled hand gentleman cake on fire
poor fellow in the street behave yourself
ugly cable dresser in my skull disco joint
for both eardrums.., there goes greeting mr big fish
where are the small fish
double adopter swivel turn wire
dangling a carrot current flow before my face
that which reminded me of my childhood friends
mpoporia en dingding dancing to the sound of a wornout
trouser rollerskate sound mamma shall we pack now
mamma miya chuchu freebees man
the meaty juice is spilling all over the tap
backoff comeover
comeover
comeover
comeover backoff

merry my babie

merry my baby

merry my baby
like whisky
jack d
whisky jack d
whisky jack d
waterfront scheme roast
jobber gate tooth face blush
cooldrinks appletiser
spicy salad curry chips drive
merry my baby
like whisky
jack d
whisky jack d
whisky jack d

smart alecs

smart alecs
lingo mix style my sister
listen now carefully
since yesterday
in the evening
i did have a lengthy chat with you
to make you understand everything
i sweetly say alright without any problems
let alone a distant buddy beauty plaster sweet nothing
you are much better of in that looks
everything from hair to toe intact no exaggeration
open and close high class act
no one is interested in others these days
to their best level
sneezer posh
i am foolishly concerned
i even go crazy
thinking about you my sister
alright fine
you sing me a song worth singing
smart alecs
is it not good enough that i sing
sister lizah madunas daughter
i will buy you bananas
i have pillow case
i have sheets and a bed also
to sleep on
in our bedroom cohesion
first floor smokers corner
plank fountain plate hovel
fix no fuss

mochochonono crazy

1 side a (i)

streamline crazy

streamline crazy
around the corner
streamline crazy
jigsaw puzzle
capsize milky way
purple light mirror in the mud
how do you operate in the dark
dirty dozen censorship heels
is both site
doctor feel good ginger cake
fine words butters no pass nips
chopper chopper chapies
mingle sweet juicy flow
on that verse wise man
on that account
side stepping
is not a coward act
neither running away
is to take a stamina buddy
they say
hang on tsotsi we are taking a turn
corners crash
travelling rugs verandha
stoep no dice
clever witty heads
we are now here
with a mum for man
hide your head you fool
crazy milky way
jigsaw puzzle
dies milky way

streamline crazy

without any fussy problems
current solo page
no waiting five tense thoughtful site caution
it's a get up and let go
radio zulu air waves
careful platform one out flying scattered papers
hardboardbox paper remain intact
time is running out home buddy
redundant stupid kite
crazy milky way
jigsaw puzzle
dance milky way
snakes and ladder banana car
free bees go away
they are selling inside meat tripes
dumplings and fat cakes
wrong site surveyor hobo stick in the mud
plus minus one problem
full of gossip about nothing
stupid blind oxen tailor
istrike now lately school bar no drakes
until each and every little bird in its own nest
or what or how do i say now lately this thoughtful site caution
well i salute you chiefs wearing the crown
sharp over my neighbourly brothers
hallo..,
crazy milky way
jigsaw puzzle
kite milky way
sweetly nice
not bad

bafoza

neighbourly one

neighbourly one
brother man
take your time steam
cool down brother man
they are plenty cats at home joe
there is no more great hall dance
now lately for the rat race
minkey mouse and mice chipping monkey soul
as much as they please
when the mother cat is away
cup shape small business teaspoon tips bottle figure
marvelous fanta mix cockeye air spirit wrong site
conscious sight puppet string cola-punch circle
go down slow cheap boaster courts of law
if you see a stop sign be aware
check short left and short right driver
javelin sports man twist no u-turn
cool down steam
cool down brother man
from the six nine station rider pee
all the way spoon down test no more coming
back joe
at home they are a lot of cats and tricks
right across the heart and soul of the city buddy
dry safely grand
by the corner peeping tom
tread your needle with care gambling stall
cool down steam
cool down brother man

dube

dube

they pick on you boys
they pick on you..,
do you fear them
no we don't fear them we want them
fear go
fair fight
fear go..,
buddy rough dance a persistent coward
playing with girls
above site wrong site there's no place
for sweet nothing bugger rol here any more
boys be boys
fear go
fair fight
fear go..,
no holding no biting fool
i hate stones machete
knife gun down
shake hands steady gongsplit
rumble roar in the jungle holy seven
fear go
fair fight
fear go..,
let alone my cheery careful saratoga express
you step on my toes its war persistent coward
playing with girls
who's next
so, so, rush over
fear go
fair fight
fear go..,

ek gaan capitol

i am going to the capitol

i am going to the capitol
for that crowning will of do
or die indeed
live like dangerous fearsome danger
we are both identical the same like siamese twins
me myself i and danger
bullish coward fear driven heart conspiracy gate
no taking chances with me
i am going to the capitol
knock knock.., who's there
or who is it
your friend
your friend who
joe nuts

inside of me

inside of me

inside of me
inside of me joe
the language stream
all assorted jolly eat and be merry
moonlight stars milkshake
huge witness above
inside of me
there is no room for cappuccino
home made brew and beers collide
causing me to vomit
inside of me joe
they are selling tripes inside meat
dumplings and fat cakes
oesophagus colour bar print slow down jabs nearby
inside of me joe
sponge lungs chicken bean bones
flat tubes archer ginger cake liquor oven grey
time tick tock ticks drum turn
fantastic orange heart beat yo yo flex
inside of me
some one is knocking passionately
to no avail
sour kidney structure four five draw
six nine appeal get by
rovers reff hum eh..,
huks free state

dollyfluit 1(ii) b side

grand whistle

tjovitjo is a grand whistle gesture
half freely covered and soothing
sharp over grand
how is it
buddy man..,
as far as i am concerned
this is my message pin
Y2K compliant
tjovitjo whistle gesture means
a soothing start
tjovitjo tswee.., lets begin

after the myth

close quote
unquote
(after all is said and done)
after the myth
stay alert
clever street lover
peter the hermit
slips tonight
open and close
my royal rod
properly fixed
witch craft lords conspirator
if you don't climb down
the branch of the tree is miracles
twine two touch golden lay migrate
small beads bare my name
my ancestors have long came together
climbers down the branch of the tree
vultures ate the elephant and
the head survived the butchers
across the church yard
in a country's dirty laundry
we buried our differences
singing go well
sleep well
thats it..,
on earth we clear
our throats and swallow

www.ingramcontent.com/pod-product-compliance
Lightning Source LLC
Chambersburg PA
CBHW050915160426
43194CB00011B/2418
* 9 7 8 0 6 3 9 8 7 8 5 1 5 *